AQA GCSE MUSIC

Listening Tests

ANDREW S. COXON &
JOHN KELLEHER

First published 2017 in Great Britain by
Rhinegold Education
14-15 Berners Street
London W1T 3LJ, UK
www.rhinegoldeducation.co.uk

© 2017 Rhinegold Education
a division of Music Sales Limited

All rights reserved. No part of this publication may be reproduced, stored in a retrieval system, or transmitted in any form or by any means, electronic, mechanical, photocopying, recording or otherwise, without the prior permission of Rhinegold Education.

Rhinegold Education has used its best efforts in preparing this guide. It does not assume, and hereby disclaims, any liability to any party for loss or damage caused by errors or omissions in the guide whether such errors or omissions result from negligence, accident or other cause.

> You should always check the current requirements of your examination, since these may change.

Editors: Lucy Metzger and Katharine Allenby
Cover and book design: Fresh Lemon Australia

AQA GCSE Music Listening Tests
Order no. RHG111
ISBN 978-1-78558-153-3

Exclusive Distributors:
Music Sales Ltd
Distribution Centre, Newmarket Road
Bury St Edmunds, Suffolk IP33 3YB, UK

Printed in the EU

Available from Rhinegold Education for your course:
- **AQA GCSE Study Guide**
- **AQA GCSE Revision Guide**

You may find the following books useful too:
- **GCSE Music Composition Workbook**
- **GCSE Music Literacy Workbook**
- **GCSE Performance Pieces:**
  Piano, Voice, Alto Sax, Clarinet, Flute, Guitar, Bass Guitar, Drums
- **Understanding Popular Music**
- **Careers in Music**
- **Music Technology from Scratch**
- **Dictionary of Music in Sound**

Contents

Introduction 5

Section A: Listening – Unfamiliar music 14

Area of Study 1:
Western Classical tradition 1650-1910 14

Area of Study 2:
Popular music 24

Area of Study 3:
Traditional music 32

Area of Study 4:
Western Classical tradition since 1910 40

How to combine questions to produce a paper worth 68 marks 48

Section B: Study pieces 50

Answers 54

Track listings 65

Glossary 68

How to download your music tracks 72

The authors

Andrew S. Coxon

graduated from York University with a degree in music and English before going on to Leeds University to complete a PGCE qualification, and later gained a further degree from the Open University.

Over a teaching career of 45 years as Head of Music, he taught Key Stage 3, GCSE, AS and A Levels in a range of comprehensive and high schools. He was involved in annual musical productions and ran a wide range of instrumental and vocal groups. His love of composing and arranging led him to write for many of the groups he organised, both in school and in the community.

Andrew has been involved in examining and moderating for many years, rising to hold senior examining positions, and has written for a variety of educational publishers.

John Kelleher

is a former school music teacher, head of department and senior leader. He is a regular contributor to *Music Teacher* magazine and has worked with a number of organisations, including Music Mark and Musical Futures.

John is a Director at Educational Social Media, which provides inbound digital marketing services to organisations who sell products and services to schools.

Introduction

This Introduction covers the following topics:
- **Using this book: for the student**
  - **The Understanding music exam**
  - **Answers**
  - **Preparing for the exam: listening practice**
  - **Exam tips and techniques**
  - **How to tackle the unfamiliar music questions**
- **Using this book: for the teacher**

Using this book: for the student

The Understanding music exam

This part of your course is worth 40% of your final GCSE marks and is assessed by an exam which is taken in June in the final year of the course. This book is designed to help you to prepare for that exam.

The exam is divided into two sections.

Section A: Listening – unfamiliar music, worth 68 marks, will contain eight questions, all linked to musical excerpts. The questions will reflect all four areas of study (AoS):

- AoS1 Western Classical tradition 1650–1910
- AoS2 Popular music
- AoS3 Traditional music
- AoS4 Western Classical tradition since 1910

You will be asked to listen to recordings of musical excerpts from each of the four areas of study. Each recording will be played a given number of times (the number of times will be shown on your exam paper). The questions will ask you to identify and describe accurately the musical elements and musical contexts, and will ask you to demonstrate your use of musical notation, including staff notation.

You will have three minutes to read through the questions before any of the excerpts are played. There will be a separate musical excerpt or set of excerpts for each question. There will be pauses between each playing and longer pauses before each new question begins, so you will have plenty of time to think about and write down your answers.

There will be a range of types of question, which will include:
- Questions asking you to identify an instrument, technique or other musical element that can be heard in the extract
- Questions showing several pitch outlines, from which the correct one is to be identified
- Questions showing several rhythmic patterns, from which the correct one is to be identified
- Questions with a notated score where the missing notes of a melody have to be added: the rhythm of the missing melody will usually be shown
- Questions asking you to specify a pitch or chord from a particular bar: bar numbers and/or notation will be shown
- Open-ended questions to be answered in one or more sentences
- Questions where two versions of the same music are to be compared.

GCSE MUSIC LISTENING TESTS

Remember that each question is directly linked to a specific area of study and individual sub-questions will focus on either an element of music or the context within which the music was written.

The aim of this book is to give you examples of the different types of musical excerpts and questions you will encounter, to point out the most common challenges and difficulties within them, and to provide valuable practice at examination-style questions.

Section B: Study pieces, worth 28 marks, will focus on the study pieces that you will have been studying throughout the course, one from each of the four areas of study.

Question 9, relating to the Western Classical tradition 1650–1910 is **compulsory**. You will choose **one** other question to answer, from questions 10 to 12, each one being based on a study piece from the three other areas of study. You will need to be able to appraise each of these pieces critically, using knowledge and understanding of:

- The effect of audience, time and place on how each of the pieces was created, developed and performed;
- How and why the music across the areas of study changed over time;
- How the composer's purpose and intention for the study pieces is reflected in their use of musical elements;
- Musical vocabulary and terminology that is relevant to the study pieces.

There will be no musical excerpts played for any of the questions on the study pieces.

Answers

The answers to all the questions in this book are given at the back of the book.

When you have completed a question to the best of your ability, check your work against the answers. Where a range of answers is possible, look at the other responses that would have gained you marks. Remember that any mark scheme is just a guide, as it is always possible that there will be other valid ways of responding to a question besides those listed. If you are in any doubt as to whether or not your own answer is deserving of credit, discuss this with your teacher.

Preparing for the exam: listening practice

Listening techniques

During the two-year GCSE course your teacher will play a lot of music from different periods, for different ensembles, in different styles and by many different composers.

A lot of it will be new to you: always try to listen with open ears and an open mind. You will be pleasantly surprised just how much music is familiar to you through its use in advertisements, in films, as theme tunes to programmes and, increasingly, as part of the sound track on computer games. It is likely that you will hear many pieces of music that you will find appealing and that might even lead you to research other pieces by the same composer, singer or group.

Learn to listen closely and critically. Here are some suggestions as to how to listen:

- Think in terms of the elements of music and use them as a basis for appraising what you hear, though not always trying to cover **every** element. Get into the habit of basing your listening around an easily remembered mnemonic such as **DR SMITH**:

    Dynamics

    Rhythm (and metre)

    Structure (and form)

    Melody

    Instruments (timbre)

    Texture

    Harmony (and tonality)

GCSE MUSIC LISTENING TESTS

- Try to identify instruments, tonalities (atonal, major, minor or modal), time signatures and/or forms.
- Listen to how different composers have used individual families of instruments:
  - String instruments, whether in chamber groups, a string orchestra or a traditional music ensemble;
  - Brass instruments, whether within an orchestra, for a fanfare, in a brass band or in a jazz band;
  - Percussion instruments, both tuned and untuned;
  - Woodwind instruments, whether in chamber groups of like instruments, in mixed woodwind groupings, in an orchestra or in a jazz band;
  - Jazz combinations, large and small; it is here that you are most likely to hear effects such as *con sordino* (with a mute) and *glissando* (slide);
  - Rock groups, listening particularly to the ways in which guitars and percussion have been used;
  - Vocal groups, both accompanied and unaccompanied (*a cappella*).
- Listen for the different effects of various instrumental techniques: for example, plucking the strings (*pizzicato*), using the bow (*arco*), playing with the wood of the bow (*col legno*), using a mute (*con sordino*), sustaining and *una corda* pedals on the piano, and so on.
- Listen also for different types of articulation: playing smoothly (*legato*), playing crisply or in a detached manner (*staccato*), the use of ornaments (such as trills, mordents or turns), changing speeds (*tempi*) through *rallentado/ritardando/ritenuto* (abbreviated to *rall.* or *rit.*) – to slow down gradually – or *accelerando* (abbreviated to *accel.*) – to speed up gradually.
- What is the texture of the piece you hear?
- Is there a particular rhythmic feature? – an ostinato? a riff? syncopation?
- Does the melody move mainly by step? by leap? through a chord? a mixture of these?
- How would you describe the accompaniment to the main melody? For example, is there an Alberti-bass pattern?
- Be aware of when the music was written and the occasion for which it might have been written. Think about how these factors influenced the outcome of the composition.

Whenever you listen to a piece of music, focus on one or more of its musical features and listen as closely and accurately as you can. Discuss your findings with others, whether in a small group or as part of the GCSE class.

Other ways in which you can prepare for the examination

Using your 'inner ear'

Everyone can 'sing' a tune inside his or her head: this is called the 'inner ear'. You need to train your 'inner ear' so that you can 'hear' in your head what a pattern of notes sounds like and so you can also 'hear' the notes you write down in response to a dictation question.

You can do this in different ways:

- Look at a short tune and try to imagine what it sounds like: think of the rhythm and the way the tune moves – up or down, by step or leap. When you have had a try, play the tune over (or get somebody else to do it for you) and see how close you were. The more you practise, the better you will get.
- Imagine a short phrase in your head and then try to write it down: to notate it. When you have had a try, play back what you have written (or get somebody else to do it for you) and see how close you were.
- Write a short pattern of notes onto a stave, using either the treble or bass clef, depending on which you read more easily. Look at what you have written in terms of rhythm and pitch and try to 'hear' it in your head. When you have tried this, as before, play back what you have written (or get somebody else to do it for you) and see how close you were.

GCSE MUSIC LISTENING TESTS

Expanding your listening

If you are an instrumentalist or a singer, explore the wider repertoire of composers whose music you come across. For example, if you are preparing for a grade examination, look for other pieces by the composers whose work you are studying.

Listen to music that you have heard before and that you know demonstrates well the use of one or more elements of music.

Listen to dance music and try to work out the characteristic rhythms that set different dances apart from each other, whether the dance is a waltz, a polka, a minuet, a club dance, disco music, and so on.

The recordings that accompany the questions in this book are short excerpts from longer pieces of music: wherever possible, try to listen to the whole of these pieces. It might open up new and exciting areas of music for you to explore.

Learning about context, vocabulary and special terms

Your teacher will give examples of how the music of different composers has been shaped by the audience and occasion for which it was written: the **context** in which it was composed. There are also a range of historical factors that influenced how composers worked, whether it was the range of notes available on instruments, the performing techniques that prevailed at the time, or the actual resources to be used.

Remember that each element of music has its own **vocabulary**: make sure you know and understand any musical **terms** that appear in the GCSE Music specification, including Italian terms for dynamics and tempo, terms for playing and singing techniques, and terms for different styles and genres of music.

Exam tips and techniques

Here are some DOs and DON'Ts to keep in mind when tackling a listening examination.

DON'T waste the three minutes' reading time at the start. Look through the paper carefully and, especially, be ready for the first question: getting off to a good start will give you confidence.

DON'T dwell on a question you feel you have not done well in: put it behind you and resolve to do well on the next one.

DON'T give a choice of answers if you are asked for a single fact and only one mark is allocated: the examiner cannot accept this and will mark your answer as incorrect, because you will have given alternative answers and it is not for the examiner to select the correct one.

DON'T leave an answer blank: at least try to have a well-informed guess within the element that forms the focus of the question. If necessary, leave a note for yourself and go back to it in the time that will remain after the final playing of the last excerpt.

DO look carefully at the mark allocation for each part of a question. This will tell you just how much detail is needed: for example, if there are two marks, then you will need to give two separate pieces of information to gain both marks. A good example of this is when you are asked to name a melodic interval: where this attracts two marks, your answer will need to be, for example, not just a **3rd** but a **major** or **minor 3rd**. However, if only **one** mark is available, you may well cancel out a correct answer by writing **major 3rd** rather than just **3rd**.

DO look carefully at the options given within a multi-choice type of answer: work out just what it is that you will have to listen for in order to be able to recognise the correct answer.

DO read the question carefully and answer exactly what you are asked. For example, a question might ask you to comment on **timbre** and **texture** as used in a particular excerpt: make sure you focus on these two elements alone, as any comments on the other elements will be ignored by the examiner as irrelevant.

DO use your 'inner ear': if you are asked to choose between different rhythms or different melodic outlines, try to work out what they sound like **in your head** and spot where the differences occur.

DO remember that each question is linked to what you can actually **hear** in the excerpt.

GCSE MUSIC LISTENING TESTS

How to tackle the unfamiliar music questions

Example question 1

What is the time signature of this excerpt? [1 mark]

You should decide first if the pulse (or beat) of the music divides by two or three. If it is two, you should next decide whether the beat divides into groups of two quavers or three. If both answers are 'two', then a range of answers will usually be permitted, including $\frac{2}{4}$, $\frac{4}{4}$, $\frac{2}{2}$, common time – **C** – and split common time – **¢**.

If the pulse is two but the quavers are grouped in threes, then the excerpt is in compound time or $\frac{6}{8}$.

If you feel that there are three beats in a bar, then a time signature of $\frac{3}{4}$ should be written, although both $\frac{3}{8}$ and $\frac{3}{2}$ are likely to be accepted.

To practise for this kind of question, you should listen to a wide range of music and try to work out the time signature. It can be useful to practise in groups, listening to pieces with different rhythms and tapping out the rhythmic elements. For example, one person could keep a steady pulse or beat while another adds two notes, or quavers, to every beat. This could then be changed so that each beat is subdivided into three.

Examples of this are given below and can be clapped or tapped out on any surface.

Example question 2

Which of the following rhythms can be heard on the snare drum at the beginning of this excerpt? Tick your answer.

[1 mark]

As part of your preparation for this type of question, work out the different rhythms in your head and also look for similarities and differences. For example, in the four patterns above, C and D start with two equal quavers but the pattern on the second beat is different – look carefully and work out the change in rhythm; A and B start with the same pattern twice, but A starts with a quaver, while B starts with two semiquavers.

Example question 3

Name or describe the cadence at the end of this excerpt. [1 mark]

The syllabus lists four cadences you are expected to be able to recognise: **perfect**, **plagal**, **imperfect** or **interrupted**. You will need to practise hearing what they sound like and how to differentiate them.

Example question 4

What is the tonality of this excerpt?
Circle your answer.

      atonal   **major**   **minor**   **modal** [1 mark]

Remember:
- Atonal music will sound as if it is not in any key at all;
- Music in a major key tends to sound bright and cheerful;
- Music in a minor key is often associated with sadder, more serious or more formal occasions (though there are examples of lively music written in a minor key such as *Badinerie* by J.S. Bach);
- Modal music can be recognised often because there is no 'leading note', no semitone, between the 7th and 8th notes of the scale;
- NB There will be occasions when this question does not take the form of a multi-choice answer.

GCSE MUSIC LISTENING TESTS

Example question 5
Describe the texture of this excerpt. [1 mark]

You need to bear in mind the different types of texture identified in the syllabus, such as **homophonic**, **polyphonic** and **imitative**, and then choose the one that best suits the excerpt you are being played. You can prepare for this type of question by listening to music that reflects the different textures mentioned.
In particular, listen carefully for the difference between music in **unison** and music played in **octaves**: in both, the melody will be played or sung by different people but, in the first, all will be at the same pitch while, in the second, some will play or sing higher and/or lower than others.

Example question 6

There will always be a question where you will have to fill in some notes omitted from the melody being played. This will usually take this form:

On the score, fill in the missing notes in bars 3 and 4, using the given rhythm.

[6 marks]

- 1 mark awarded per correct pitch
- Award 1 mark for the correct shape, regardless of starting note

This is the correct answer:

This type of question tests your ability to hear the way in which a short melody moves and then to write the notes onto the stave. Being able to use musical notation or staff notation is a requirement of the syllabus, and this is one way in which both that knowledge and your ability to hear different pitches can be tested.

In this type of question, always use the last note **before** the notes you have to fill in, and the note that comes **after** the last note you will add, as reference points for the pitch. The excerpt is likely to be played five times to give you plenty of opportunity to work out the correct pitches. Make sure that you write them clearly so that there cannot be any doubt whether your notes are in a space or on a line: if it isn't clear, you will not get the mark.

In this case, the first note you add is on the **same pitch** (A) as the last written note and the last note you will add is an E, the **same pitch** as the written note that follows. Using this information from the score can help you check the notes you have added in.

Notice also that, in this case, all the notes move by step from one note to the next: this might not always be the case, but there will never be any big leaps. If you think the notes haven't moved by step, sing from one to the next *in your head* counting the steps. For example, if the notes are a 3rd apart, you would think C D E (or whatever the three notes would be), singing the three pitches in your head and, if necessary, don't be ashamed to use your fingers to count!

GCSE MUSIC LISTENING TESTS

Example question 7

Describe the dynamics at the beginning of this excerpt. [1 mark]

To answer this, you can use Italian terms such as *forte* or *piano*; you can use their abbreviations – *f* or *p*; or you can simply describe the dynamic using English words – loud or quiet. Note that, in this case, it is the dynamic levels **at the beginning of the excerpt** that are the focus of the question.

In some cases, you might be asked to give the Italian term or you might be asked to choose from a list of dynamics using Italian terms or their abbreviations. Read the question carefully before answering.

Example question 8

Name the melody instrument heard at the beginning of this excerpt. [1 mark]

This tests your ability to recognise a particular instrumental timbre. You should practise for this type of question by listening to a wide range of music and trying to identify the different instruments involved. Notice that this question is focussed on a melody instrument – an instrument that can play different pitches – so ignore any unpitched percussion instruments you might hear.

A question might also be set asking you to identify a family or group (ensemble) of instruments or even a playing/performance technique (such as *pizzicato*, plucking the strings, or *con sordino*, with a mute).

Example question 9

Which of the following best fits the structure of this excerpt?
Circle your answer:

    AABA   ABCA   AABC   ABCD [1 mark]

For this type of question, listen to the excerpt and try to recognise when a phrase or melody returns. If there are contrasting sections, where do they come? Again, use any preparation time to note the similarities and differences between the different patterns.

With the four patterns given above, two start with the first section (Section A) coming twice, the other two start with Section A once followed by a contrast (Section B). If you hear two different sections, you then have to decide if, after a third new section (C), the music goes back to the start (Section A) or adds in yet another new section (D).

Start by deciding which of these patterns is correct up to the first two letters and then you can narrow down your choice to two options rather than four.

Using this book: for the teacher

There is a range of ways in which the questions in this book can be used.

- Each of the 34 listening questions in this book contains several parts. You could base a lesson on one of the questions, discussing the various terms, references and musical elements that are the focus of the individual parts. Students could suggest other ways in which they have used or encountered the various features – such as a rhythmic figure, a cadence, a modulation, a specific instrumental/vocal timbre, a particular ensemble, and so on. Ideas could be shared on how to recognise the different features within the excerpt.
- You might set a question for homework or extension work.
- In the actual examination, each excerpt will have a range of questions based on it and the recording will be played several times (two, three, four, even five). This book indicates how many times an excerpt should be played, but, if necessary and especially during the earlier practice stages, additional repetitions should be allowed.
- You could use an individual question to improve exam technique and the ability to respond to the questions with the recording played the correct number of times. Where this is done, time should be allowed to read through the question – the time given in the exam will be three minutes – and then the excerpt should be played the given number of times, with pauses of about 20 to 30 seconds in between.
- You might set a small group of questions as a 'mini' mock examination to check the progress of your students' knowledge and understanding. Perhaps two or four questions could be selected, based either on a single area of study or on two areas with two questions for each, or taking one from each area of study. The questions should be chosen to cover the different types of questions that will be encountered – including one where missing notes of a melody have to be written in, one where a rhythm is to be recognised, one without any musical notation at all and one that includes some extended writing. Three minutes should be allowed for reading through each question and a pause of about one minute given between questions.
- On pages 48-49 you will find suggestions on how to select combinations of questions to produce a balanced paper that will add up to a total of **68** marks, thus matching the total that will be awarded for Section A of the Understanding Music paper. Section B questions are provided separately, for the remaining **28** marks.

Audio

All the audio you will need to do these tests is provided via the download card that is included in the back of this book. Instructions on how to download the tracks are given there. Please note that the code on the card can only be used once: save the downloaded tracks somewhere safe!

Section A: Listening – unfamiliar music

AREA OF STUDY 1:
Western Classical tradition 1650–1910

Question 1

This excerpt will be played five times.

You may find it helpful to tick a box each time you hear the excerpt.

☐ ☐ ☐ ☐ ☐

The rhythm of the excerpt is provided below.

1. Name the instrument playing the melody in this excerpt.

   _____ [1 mark]

2. Name the types of cadence marked *w* and *x* in the rhythmic outline above.

   Cadence *w* _____ [1 mark]

   Cadence *x* _____ [1 mark]

3. Name the intervals marked *y* and *z* in the rhythmic outline above.

   Interval *y* _____ [1 mark]

   Interval *z* _____ [1 mark]

4. What is the tonality of this excerpt?

   _____ [1 mark]

5. Identify **three** features of melody and harmony typical of the music of the Classical period that you can hear in this excerpt.

   _____
   _____
   _____

   [3 marks]

   Total: 9 marks

SECTION A: UNFAMILIAR MUSIC

Question 2

This excerpt will be played five times.

You may find it helpful to tick a box each time you hear the excerpt.

☐ ☐ ☐ ☐ ☐

1. Which **three** of the following melodic devices are featured in this excerpt? Circle your answers.

   acciaccatura   appoggiatura   anacrusis

   chromatic movement   diminution   glissando

   inversion   triadic movement

   [3 marks]

2. The excerpt begins in G minor. In which key does it end?

   _____

   [1 mark]

3. On which note of the scale does this excerpt begin? Circle your answer.

   1st   3rd   5th   7th

   [1 mark]

4. Which Italian term best describes the tempo of this music?

   _____

   [1 mark]

5. What is the time signature of this excerpt?

   _____

   [1 mark]

6. Name the type of cadence at the end of the excerpt.

   _____

   [1 mark]

7. What name is normally given to this group of instruments?

   _____

   [1 mark]

Total: 9 marks

Question 3

This excerpt will be played five times.

You may find it helpful to tick a box each time you hear the excerpt.

☐ ☐ ☐ ☐ ☐

1. Name the instrument playing the melody in this excerpt.

_____

[1 mark]

2. On the score, fill in the missing notes in **bars 3–4** using the given rhythm.

[6 marks]

3. Which musical term or phrase best describes the texture of this excerpt?

_____

[1 mark]

4. What is the tonality at the end of this excerpt?

_____

[1 mark]

Total: 9 marks

Question 4

This excerpt will be played five times.
You may find it helpful to tick a box each time you hear the excerpt.

☐ ☐ ☐ ☐ ☐

1. Name the instrument playing the melody in this excerpt.

   _____ [1 mark]

2. Name **two** melodic ornaments heard during this excerpt.

   _____
   _____ [2 marks]

3. Which musical term or phrase best describes the texture of this excerpt?

   _____ [1 mark]

4. Which families of instruments play the accompaniment in this excerpt?

   _____ [1 mark]

5. Which Italian term best describes the tempo of this music?

   _____ [1 mark]

6. What is the time signature of this excerpt?

   _____ [1 mark]

7. Name the type of cadence at the end of the excerpt.

   _____ [1 mark]

8. This music starts in the tonic key: in which key does the excerpt end?
   Tick your answer.

   ☐ tonic

   ☐ subdominant

   ☐ dominant

   ☐ relative minor [1 mark]

   Total: 9 marks

GCSE MUSIC LISTENING TESTS

Question 5

This excerpt will be played four times.
You may find it helpful to tick a box each time you hear the excerpt.

☐ ☐ ☐ ☐

1. Which of the following best fits the type of choir singing this excerpt?
Circle your answer.

    ATBB   **SATB**   **SSAA**   **TTBB**

[1 mark]

2. Which **two** of the following best describe the texture of this excerpt?
Circle your answers.

    a cappella   **antiphonal**   **contrapuntal**

    homophonic   **imitative**

[2 marks]

3. Which of the following patterns best matches the vocal line sung at the beginning of this excerpt? Tick your answer.

A ☐
B ☐
C ☐
D ☐

[1 mark]

4. Which of the following patterns best matches the vocal line sung later during this excerpt? Tick your answer.

A ☐
B ☐
C ☐
D ☐

[1 mark]

5. Identify **three** features of harmony and instrumentation used in this excerpt that are typical of Baroque music.

_____

_____

_____

[3 marks]

Total: 8 marks

SECTION A: UNFAMILIAR MUSIC

Question 6

This excerpt will be played four times.

You may find it helpful to tick a box each time you hear the excerpt.

☐ ☐ ☐ ☐

1. The first of the two short sections of this excerpt is slow. Which of the following best describes its opening chord? Tick your answer.

   ☐ major

   ☐ minor

   ☐ dominant 7th [1 mark]

2. This is the rhythm of the first section. Describe the melodic movement in **bars 4–7**.

   _____

   _____

   _____ [3 marks]

3. Describe the tempo of the second section of this excerpt.

   _____ [1 mark]

4. Which **one** of the following best describes the texture of this excerpt? Circle your answer.

   antiphonal   homophonic   monophonic   octaves [1 mark]

5. Name the type of cadence at the end of this excerpt.

   _____ [1 mark]

6. What is the tonality at the end of this excerpt?

   _____ [1 mark]

7. Which of the following best matches the dynamics at the beginning and end of this excerpt? Tick your answer.

A	beginning p	end p	☐
B	beginning p	end f	☐
C	beginning f	end f	☐
D	beginning f	end p	☐

   [1 mark]

   Total: 9 marks

Question 7

This excerpt will be played five times.

You may find it helpful to tick a box each time you hear the excerpt.

1. Name the type of cadence played in bar 4 as marked in the skeleton score below.

   _____

   [1 mark]

2. This is a skeleton score of the first eight bars of this excerpt.
   Complete the melody in **bars 7–8** using the given rhythm.

   [5 marks]

3. Which of the following best fits the form of this excerpt?
   Circle your answer.

   AABBAA   A¹A²BB A¹A²   A¹A²B¹B²A¹A²   AABCAA

   [1 mark]

4. Describe **two** features of articulation used in the playing of this excerpt.

   _____

   _____

   [2 marks]

   Total: 9 marks

SECTION A: UNFAMILIAR MUSIC

Question 8

This excerpt will be played four times.

You may find it helpful to tick a box each time you hear the excerpt.

☐ ☐ ☐ ☐

1. Name the interval between the first two notes of the melody of this excerpt.

   _____
   [2 marks]

2. Which of the following rhythms best matches that of the melody's opening phrase? Tick your answer.

   A ♩ | ♫ ♩. ♪ | ♩

   B ♩ | ♩.♪ ♩. ♪ | ♩

   C ♩ | ♫ ♩ ♩ | ♩

   D ♩ | ♩.♫ ♩ | ♩

   ☐
   ☐
   ☐
   ☐
   [1 mark]

3. Which of the following chords is heard at the end of the opening phrase? Tick your answer.

   ☐ major

   ☐ minor

   ☐ dominant 7th

   [1 mark]

4. Which Italian term best describes the tempo of this excerpt?

   _____
   [1 mark]

5. Which **two** of the following rhythmic features are used in this excerpt? Circle your answers.

   augmentation   **hemiola**   **rallentando**

   rubato   **triplets**
   [2 marks]

6. What is the tonality of this excerpt?

   _____
   [1 mark]

Total: 8 marks

GCSE MUSIC LISTENING TESTS

Question 9

This excerpt will be played five times.
You may find it helpful to tick a box each time you hear the excerpt.

1. Describe the texture of this excerpt.

   _____

   [1 mark]

2. Which melodic ornament can be heard during this excerpt?

   _____

   [1 mark]

3. On which note of the scale does **bar 7** end? Circle your answer.

   1st   **3rd**   **5th**   **7th**

   [1 mark]

4. Below is an outline of the melody of this excerpt.
   Complete the melody in **bars 11–12** using the given rhythm.

   [5 marks]

5. Which of the following best describes the type of articulation used in this excerpt?
   Circle your answer.

   accented   **legato**   **marcato**   **staccato**

   [1 mark]

   Total: 9 marks

SECTION A: UNFAMILIAR MUSIC

Question 10

This excerpt will be played five times.

You may find it helpful to tick a box each time you hear the excerpt.

☐ ☐ ☐ ☐ ☐

1. Name the keyboard instrument that can be heard in the short introduction to this excerpt.

   _____
   [1 mark]

2. Which of the following types of voice is singing at the beginning of this excerpt? Circle your answer

   soprano   **alto**   **tenor**   **bass**   [1 mark]

3. Below is a skeleton score of this excerpt beginning with the entry of the voices. Complete the melody in **bars 6–7** using the given rhythm.

   [6 marks]

4. What happens to the dynamics after the first note shown in bar 8 above?

   _____
   [1 mark]

   Total: 9 marks

AREA OF STUDY 2:
Popular music

Question 11

This excerpt will be played five times.

You may find it helpful to tick a box each time you hear the excerpt.

☐ ☐ ☐ ☐ ☐

1. Name the keyboard instrument accompanying the vocal melody at the beginning of this excerpt.

   _____

   [1 mark]

2. Describe the melodic movement of the first three notes of the vocal line in this excerpt.

   _____

   _____

   [2 marks]

3. Name a melodic ornament used in this excerpt.

   _____

   [1 mark]

4. What is the time signature of this excerpt?

   _____

   [1 mark]

5. Name an orchestral family that is later added to the accompaniment.

   _____

   [1 mark]

6. Identify **three** features of melody and vocal timbre typical of Broadway musicals of the 1950s to 1990s.

   _____

   _____

   _____

   [3 marks]

Total: 9 marks

SECTION A: UNFAMILIAR MUSIC

Question 12

This excerpt will be played five times.

You may find it helpful to tick a box each time you hear the excerpt.

☐ ☐ ☐ ☐ ☐

1. The vocal melody opens with four different notes as outlined below.

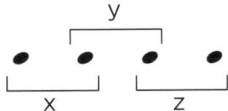

Name the intervals marked *x*, *y* and *z*.

Interval *x* _____ [1 mark]

Interval *y* _____ [1 mark]

Interval *z* _____ [1 mark]

2. Which instruments are doubling the vocal melody at the beginning of this excerpt?

_____ [1 mark]

3. Name the playing technique used by the strings in this excerpt.

_____ [1 mark]

4. What is the time signature of this excerpt?

_____ [1 mark]

5. Name **one** percussion instrument heard during this excerpt.

_____ [1 mark]

6. On which note of the scale does the vocal melody in this excerpt end?
   Circle your answer.

   1st   3rd   5th   7th   [1 mark]

Total: 8 marks

GCSE MUSIC LISTENING TESTS

Question 13

This excerpt will be played five times.

You may find it helpful to tick a box each time you hear the excerpt.

☐ ☐ ☐ ☐ ☐

1. Which of the following patterns best matches the notes played by the guitar in the opening bars? Tick your answer. [1 mark]

A  ☐   C  ☐

B  ☐   D  ☐

2. How many times is this pattern played before it changes pitch?

_____

[1 mark]

3. This opening pattern contains three different chords: how many of them are major?

_____

[1 mark]

4. Which **two** of the following are features of this opening repeated pattern?
   Circle your answers.

   finger-picking   **glissando**   **palm muting**

   pitch bend   **power chords**

[2 marks]

5. Each of the numbered boxes represents **one bar** of the music, which is in $\frac{4}{4}$.
   Put the following letters into the correct bar to show where each of these features is heard:

   w = first entry of the voice

   x = drum break

   y = entry of backing vocals

   z = a vocal note sustained by the lead vocalist across two bars (indicate either bar)

1	2	3	4	5	6	7	8
9	10	11	12	13	14	15	16

excerpt continues

[4 marks]

Total: 9 marks

SECTION A: UNFAMILIAR MUSIC

Question 14

This excerpt will be played five times.

You may find it helpful to tick a box each time you hear the excerpt.

☐ ☐ ☐ ☐ ☐

1. Name the wind instruments playing during the opening bars of this excerpt.

   _____
   [1 mark]

2. Which of the following best describes the guitar-playing technique used during these bars? Circle your answer.

   broken chords   **detached chords**

   strummed chords   **sustained chords**
   [1 mark]

3. Describe the tempo/speed of this excerpt.

   _____
   [1 mark]

4. The opening of the vocal melody has this rhythm:

   Describe the melodic movement of this section.

   _____
   [1 mark]

5. If the first note of this section of vocal melody is A, what is the final note?

   _____
   [1 mark]

6. During the vocal section, part of the guitar accompaniment is made up of a line moving in this rhythm:

   Which **two** of the following best describe the way in which these notes move? Circle your answers.

   ascending   **chromatic**   **descending**

   diatonic   **disjunct**
   [2 marks]

7. What is the tonality of this excerpt?

   _____
   [1 mark]

Total: 8 marks

Question 15

You will hear two excerpts.
Each excerpt will be played three times.

Excerpt A

You may find it helpful to tick a box each time you hear the excerpt.

☐ ☐ ☐

1. Name the instrument playing the melody during the opening bars of this excerpt.

   _____ [1 mark]

2. Which family of instruments is accompanying the melody? Circle your answer.

   woodwinds   **brass**   **strings**   **percussion**   [1 mark]

3. Describe the tempo / speed of this excerpt.

   _____ [1 mark]

4. Name **two** melodic ornaments heard in this melody.

   _____

   _____ [2 marks]

Excerpt B

You may find it helpful to tick a box each time you hear the excerpt.

☐ ☐ ☐

5. What is the time signature of the majority of this excerpt?

   _____ [1 mark]

6. Which of the following best describes the piano accompaniment?
   Circle your answer.

   arpeggios   **broken chords**   **detached chords**   **sustained chords**   [1 mark]

7. On which note of the scale does the melody begin? Circle your answer.

   1st   **3rd**   **5th**   **7th**   [1 mark]

8. What is the tonality of this excerpt?

   _____ [1 mark]

Total: 9 marks

SECTION A: UNFAMILIAR MUSIC

Question 16

This excerpt will be played five times.

You may find it helpful to tick a box each time you hear the excerpt.

☐ ☐ ☐ ☐ ☐

1. Which type of choir is singing this excerpt? Circle your answer.

   boys' choir   **ladies' choir**   **male voice choir**   **mixed voice choir**   [1 mark]

2. Which **two** of the following best describe the texture of this excerpt?
   Circle your answers.

   a cappella   **imitative**   **octaves**

   polyphonic   **unison**   [2 marks]

3. On the score below, complete the melody in **bars 5–6** using the given rhythm.

[6 marks]

Total: 9 marks

GCSE MUSIC LISTENING TESTS

Question 17

This excerpt will be played five times.

You may find it helpful to tick a box each time you hear the excerpt.

☐ ☐ ☐ ☐ ☐

1. At the beginning of the excerpt, the word 'fall' is sung four times. Comment on the use of melody and texture in this section.

   _____

   _____

   _____

   _____

   _____

   [5 marks]

2. What is the tonality of this excerpt?

   _____

   [1 mark]

3. On which beats of the bar does the side drum mostly play?

   _____

   [1 mark]

4. Name **one** keyboard instrument heard during this excerpt.

   _____

   [1 mark]

5. What is the time signature of this excerpt?

   _____

   [1 mark]

   Total: 9 marks

SECTION A: UNFAMILIAR MUSIC

Question 18

You will hear two excerpts.

Excerpt A

This excerpt will be played four times.

You may find it helpful to tick a box each time you hear the excerpt.

☐ ☐ ☐ ☐

1. Which instrument is heard at the beginning of this excerpt?

   _____

   [1 mark]

2. Hand-claps are added to the texture. Complete the following bar to show the rhythm they play.

   [4 marks]

3. Describe the texture of this excerpt?

   _____

   [1 mark]

Excerpt B

This excerpt will be played three times.

You may find it helpful to tick a box each time you hear the excerpt.

☐ ☐ ☐

4. This song has been described as 'an urgent, pounding, almost bluesy anthem': identify **three** features of rhythm, melody, dynamics and/or the use of instruments and voices that is typical of this style.

   _____

   _____

   _____

   _____

   [3 marks]

Total: 9 marks

AREA OF STUDY 3:
Traditional music

Question 19

This excerpt will be played five times.
You may find it helpful to tick a box each time you hear the excerpt.

☐ ☐ ☐ ☐ ☐

1. Which **three** of the following melodic devices are featured in this excerpt?
   Circle your answers.

   augmentation   blue notes   descant   diminution

   inversion   melisma   raga   riff

   [3 marks]

2. What name is given to the chord progression used in this excerpt?

   _____

   [1 mark]

3. Which instrument is providing the accompaniment in this excerpt?

   _____

   [1 mark]

4. Describe the rhythmic feel of this excerpt.

   _____

   [1 mark]

5. What is the time signature of this excerpt?

   _____

   [1 mark]

6. Which guitar technique is used during the lyric 'sweet home Chicago'?

   _____

   [1 mark]

Total: 8 marks

SECTION A: UNFAMILIAR MUSIC

Question 20

This excerpt will be played five times.

You may find it helpful to tick a box each time you hear the excerpt.

☐ ☐ ☐ ☐ ☐

1. The chart below shows the chord progression used throughout this excerpt.

bar 1	bar 2	bar 3	bar 4
C E⁷	major, minor or dominant 7th?	Dm A⁷	major, minor or dominant 7th?

bar 5	bar 6	bar 7	bar 8
F F♯dim	C A⁷	major, minor or dominant 7th?	D⁷ G⁷ or D⁷ C

Identify the chords in bars 2, 4 and 7 as major, minor or dominant 7th.

bar 2 _____

bar 4 _____

bar 7 _____ [3 marks]

2. What name is given to the kind of ensemble playing this excerpt?

_____ [1 mark]

3. Which instrumental technique is used by the trumpet player during his/her solo?

_____ [1 mark]

4. Describe the rhythmic feel of this excerpt.

_____ [1 mark]

5. What is the time signature of this excerpt?

_____ [1 mark]

6. What is the speed/tempo of this excerpt?

_____ [1 mark]

Total: 8 marks

Question 21

This excerpt will be played five times.

You may find it helpful to tick a box each time you hear the excerpt.

☐ ☐ ☐ ☐ ☐

1. Which technology effect has been used on the lead vocals in this recording?

   _____

   [1 mark]

2. Which **two** of the following terms best describe the playing of the electric guitar in this excerpt? Circle your answers.

       arpeggio   **pitch bend**   **hammer-on**   **muting**   **skank**

   [2 marks]

3. Describe the drum beat in this excerpt.

   _____

   [1 mark]

4. Which term best describes the style/genre of this piece of music?

   _____

   [1 mark]

5. Describe the texture and performance techniques used by the lead singer and backing vocalists in this excerpt.

   _____

   _____

   _____

   _____

   [3 marks]

   Total: 8 marks

SECTION A: UNFAMILIAR MUSIC

Question 22

This excerpt will be played five times.

You may find it helpful to tick a box each time you hear the excerpt.

☐ ☐ ☐ ☐ ☐

1. Which **one** of the following best describes the texture of the excerpt?
   Circle your answer.

   a cappella   improvised   monophonic   tutti   [1 mark]

2. In the melody in this excerpt, which **two** of the following terms best describe the melody writing in the excerpt? Circle your answers.

   anacrusis   blue notes   call and response

   melisma   pentatonic   whole tone   [2 marks]

3. Describe the tonality of this excerpt.

   _____   [1 mark]

4. Which technology effect has been applied to this recording?

   _____   [1 mark]

5. The English-language lyrics to this excerpt are:

   1   She's a rich girl, she don't try to hide it
   2   She's got diamonds on the soles of her shoes
   3   He's a poor boy, empty as a pocket
   4   Empty as a pocket but nothing to lose
   5   Sing, te-na-na, te-na-na-na
   6   She's got diamonds on the soles of her shoes
   7   Te-na-na, te-na-na-na
   8   She's got diamonds on the soles of her shoes
   9   Diamonds on the soles of her shoes
   10 Diamonds on the soles of her shoes
   11 Diamonds on the soles of her shoes
   12 Diamonds on the soles of her shoes

   Which **one** of the following terms best describes the texture for lines 9-12?
   Circle your answer.

   homophonic   monophonic   polyphonic   unison   [1 mark]

6. Identify **three** features of **rhythm** and/or **timbre** used in this excerpt that are typical of African fusion music.

   _____

   _____

   _____   [3 marks]

Total: 9 marks

Question 23

This excerpt will be played four times.
You may find it helpful to tick a box each time you hear the excerpt.

☐ ☐ ☐ ☐

1. Which **one** of the following terms best describes the tonality in this excerpt? Circle your answers.

    atonal   **major**   **minor**   **modal**

    [1 mark]

2. Which **two** of the following terms best describe the way the opening chords in this excerpt are played? Circle your answers.

    detached   **legato**   **regular beat**   **sustained**   **syncopated**

    [2 marks]

3. Which instruments play the melody which follows this introduction?

    _____

    [1 mark]

4. To which family of instruments do they belong?

    _____

    [1 mark]

5. Identify **three** features of instrumentation typical of contemporary Latin music which can be heard during this excerpt.

    _____

    _____

    _____

    [3 marks]

Total: 8 marks

SECTION A: UNFAMILIAR MUSIC

Question 24

This excerpt will be played five times.

You may find it helpful to tick a box each time you hear the excerpt.

☐ ☐ ☐ ☐ ☐

1. Which term best describes the tonality of this excerpt?

   _____

   [1 mark]

2. Which **three** terms best describe the bassline in this excerpt? Circle your answers.

   anacrusis   arpeggio   drone   melisma

   modal   shuffle   son   sequence

   [3 marks]

3. Which term best describes the texture of this excerpt?

   _____

   [1 mark]

4. Which **three** of the following instruments can be heard in this extract? Circle your answers.

   accordion   castanets   drum kit   electric guitar

   flute   saxophone   trumpet   violin

   [3 marks]

   Total: 8 marks

GCSE MUSIC LISTENING TESTS

Question 25

This excerpt will be played five times.

You may find it helpful to tick a box each time you hear the excerpt.

☐ ☐ ☐ ☐ ☐

1. Which **two** of the following best describe the instrumental melody at the beginning of this excerpt? Circle your answers.

   arpeggio　　**ascending**　　**descending**　　**disjunct**　　**scale**　　[2 marks]

2. Which **one** of the following best describes the tonality of this excerpt? Circle your answer.

   atonal　　**major**　　**minor**　　**modal**　　[1 mark]

3. The lyrics heard after the instrumental introduction are:

   Corrupted by the simple sniff of riches blown
   I know you have felt much more love than you've shown
   I'm on my knees and the water creeps to my chest.

The first and second verses follow: their lyrics are printed below.

first verse	second verse
Plant your hope with good seeds, Don't cover yourself with thistle and weeds. Rain down, rain down on me.	Look over your hills and be still, The sky above us shoots to kill. Rain down, rain down on me.

Referring to **dynamics** and **timbre**, identify **three** ways in which the musical setting differs between the first and second verse.

_____

_____

_____

[3 marks]

4. Which **one** of the following best describes the texture of this excerpt? Circle your answer.

   melody and accompaniment　　**imitative**　　**monophonic**　　**polyphonic**　　[1 mark]

5. Identify **two** ways in which the vocal line for the phrase 'rain down' emphasises the meaning of the words.

_____

_____

[2 marks]

Total: 9 marks

SECTION A: UNFAMILIAR MUSIC

Question 26

This excerpt will be played four times.

You may find it helpful to tick a box each time you hear the excerpt.

☐ ☐ ☐ ☐

1. Which **three** of the following best describe the performance techniques used by the violin in this excerpt? Circle your answers.

   arco   glissando   col legno   con sordino

   double-stopping   pizzicato   spiccato   tremolo

   [3 marks]

2. Describe how the tempo changes in the introduction to this excerpt.

   _____

   [1 mark]

3. How many different chords can be heard in this excerpt?

   _____

   [1 mark]

4. Which instrument plays the chordal accompaniment for the singer in this excerpt?

   _____

   [1 mark]

5. Which of the following best describes the tonality of this excerpt? Circle your answer.

   atonal   major   minor   modal

   [1 mark]

6. Describe the texture of this excerpt.

   _____

   [1 mark]

Total: 8 marks

AREA OF STUDY 4:
Western Classical tradition since 1910

Question 27

You will hear two excerpts.

Excerpt A

This excerpt will be played three times.

You may find it helpful to tick a box each time you hear the excerpt.

☐ ☐ ☐

1. Name the instruments playing the melody at the beginning of this excerpt.

   _____

   [1 mark]

2. Name a percussion instrument playing during this excerpt.

   _____

   [1 mark]

3. This excerpt uses two different time signatures. One is $\frac{4}{4}$: what is the other?

   _____

   [1 mark]

4. Which **two** of the following are heard in the melody line? Circle your answers.

   glissando   staccato   syncopation   trill   turn

   [2 marks]

Excerpt B

This excerpt will be played three times.

You may find it helpful to tick a box each time you hear the excerpt.

☐ ☐ ☐

5. From this excerpt, identify **four** features of harmony, melody and/or use of instruments typical of Western Classical music since 1910.

   _____

   _____

   _____

   _____

   [4 marks]

Total: 9 marks

SECTION A: UNFAMILIAR MUSIC

Question 28

This excerpt will be played five times.

You may find it helpful to tick a box each time you hear the excerpt.

☐ ☐ ☐ ☐ ☐

1. Which **two** families of instruments can be heard in this excerpt? Circle your answers

    brass   keyboard   percussion   strings   woodwind

    [2 marks]

2. Describe the dynamics in this excerpt.

    _____

    _____

    _____

    [2 marks]

3. A partial score of the melody in this excerpt is shown below

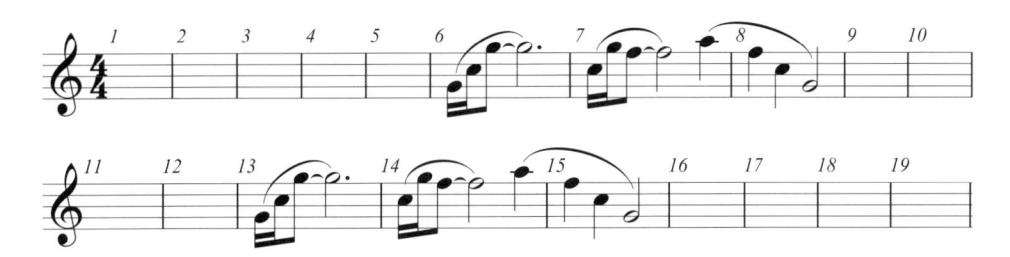

    Identify **two** ways in which the **melody** in bars 9–12 differs from that in bars 16–19.

    _____

    _____

    _____

    [2 marks]

4. Identify **two** features that would make this piece suitable for a military ceremonial occasion.

    _____

    _____

    _____

    [2 marks]

    Total: 8 marks

Question 29

You will hear two excerpts.

Excerpt A

This excerpt will be played three times.

You may find it helpful to tick a box each time you hear the excerpt.

☐ ☐ ☐

1. Name the instrument playing the melody from the beginning of this excerpt.

_____ [1 mark]

2. This excerpt begins with the chords D major and G major. Name the next chord.

_____ [1 mark]

3. Name the instruments which take over the melody.

_____ [1 mark]

4. What is the speed/tempo of this excerpt?

_____ [1 mark]

Excerpt B

This excerpt will be played four times.

You may find it helpful to tick a box each time you hear the excerpt.

☐ ☐ ☐ ☐

5. Which **two** of the following rhythmic features are heard during this excerpt?
Circle your answers.

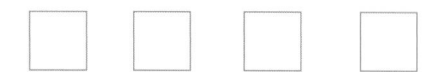

    dotted rhythms   **hemiola**   **quavers**   **rubato**   **semibreves**   [2 marks]

6. Which of the following outlines best fits the opening melody of the opening phrase?
Tick your answer. [1 mark]

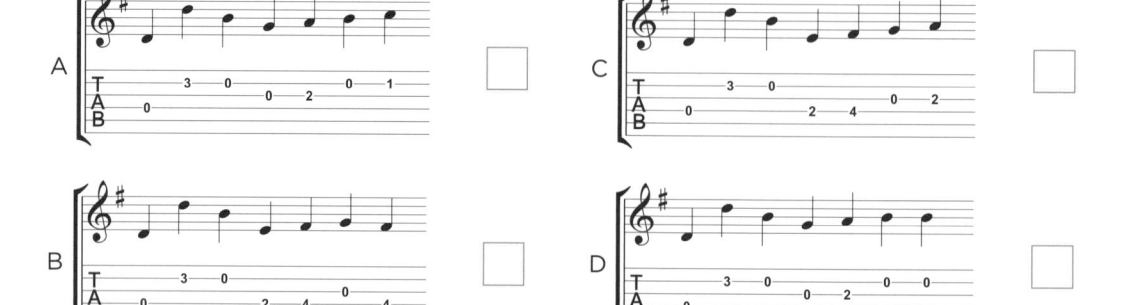

A ☐   C ☐

B ☐   D ☐

7. Which of the following best fits the form of this excerpt? Circle your answer.

    A¹A²A³A⁴   A¹A²A³B   A¹A²B¹B²   A¹B¹A²B²   [1 mark]

Total: 8 marks

Question 30

This excerpt will be played four times.

You may find it helpful to tick a box each time you hear the excerpt.

☐ ☐ ☐ ☐

1. Name the instrument that plays an ascending pattern at the beginning of this excerpt.

   _____ [1 mark]

2. Which **one** of the following harmonic devices can be heard in the opening of this excerpt?

       modulation   pedal   suspension   tièrce de picardie   [1 mark]

3. Which **one** of the following melodic devices can be heard after the opening ascending pattern has been heard for a second time? Circle your answer.

       imitation   inversion   ostinato   sequence   [1 mark]

4. What happens to the tempo during this excerpt?

   _____

   _____ [2 marks]

5. What happens to the dynamics during this excerpt?

   _____

   _____ [2 marks]

6. What name is given to this kind of instrumental ensemble?

   _____ [1 mark]

Total: 8 marks

Question 31

This excerpt will be played four times.

You may find it helpful to tick a box each time you hear the excerpt.

☐ ☐ ☐ ☐

1. Which instrument plays the melody in this excerpt?

   _____

   [1 mark]

2. Which **two** instrumental performance techniques are used by the strings in this excerpt? Circle your answers.

   arco   col legno   con sordino   pizzicato   tremolo

   [2 marks]

3. Which **one** of the following Italian terms best describes the tempo of this excerpt? Circle your answer.

   allegro   largo   moderato   vivace

   [1 mark]

4. Identify the rhythmic device used by the strings and piano in this excerpt.

   _____

   [1 mark]

5. Which **one** of the following terms best describes the musical device used by the brass in this excerpt? Circle your answer.

   drone   inversion   ostinato   sequence

   [1 mark]

6. Identify **two** features of **harmony** and **rhythm** used in this excerpt that are typical of Western Classical music since 1910.

   _____

   _____

   [2 marks]

   Total: 8 marks

SECTION A: UNFAMILIAR MUSIC

Question 32

You will hear two excerpts.

Excerpt A

This excerpt will be played four times.

You may find it helpful to tick a box each time you hear the excerpt.

☐ ☐ ☐ ☐

1. Which family of instruments plays the first four notes of this excerpt?

   _____

   [1 mark]

2. What happens to the dynamics on the fourth note?

   _____

   _____

   [2 marks]

3. Name the instrument that then plays the melody.

   _____

   [1 mark]

4. Name **two** playing techniques used by the instruments accompanying this melody.

   _____

   _____

   [2 marks]

Excerpt B

This excerpt will be played three times.

You may find it helpful to tick a box each time you hear the excerpt.

☐ ☐ ☐

5. Identify **three** features of **rhythm**, **melody** and / or **use of instruments** typical of Eastern European music and the orchestral music of Kodály.

   _____

   _____

   _____

   _____

   _____

   [3 marks]

Total: 9 marks

GCSE MUSIC LISTENING TESTS

Question 33

This excerpt will be played four times.

You may find it helpful to tick a box each time you hear the excerpt.

☐ ☐ ☐ ☐

1. What name is given to this style/genre of music?

_____

[1 mark]

2. Which **two** of the following guitar performance techniques can be heard in this excerpt? Circle your answers.

    palm-muting   picking   power chords   strumming   tapping

[2 marks]

3. Describe the texture of this excerpt.

_____

[1 mark]

4. Which technology has allowed one performer to play all the parts heard in this excerpt?

_____

[1 mark]

5. Describe the tempo/speed of this excerpt.

_____

[1 mark]

6. Identify **two** features of melody and/or timbre used in this excerpt that are typical of Western Classical music since 1910.

_____

_____

[2 marks]

Total: 8 marks

Question 34

This excerpt will be played four times.
You may find it helpful to tick a box each time you hear the excerpt.

☐ ☐ ☐ ☐

1. Which family of instruments plays this excerpt?

_____

[1 mark]

2. Name **two** playing techniques heard during this excerpt.

_____

_____

[2 marks]

3. Which of the following best matches the dynamics at the beginning and end of this excerpt? Tick your answer.

A	beginning p	end p	☐
B	beginning p	end f	☐
C	beginning f	end f	☐
D	beginning f	end p	☐

[1 mark]

4. Referring to **melody**, **harmony** and **rhythm**, give **four** ways in which this excerpt is typical of minimalist music.

_____

_____

_____

_____

[4 marks]

Total: 8 marks

How to combine questions to produce a paper worth 68 marks

As well as choosing questions that will produce a total of 68 marks, there are two other considerations to be borne in mind:

1. The two questions chosen for each Area of Study must total 17 marks, i.e. 9 + 8.
2. Within the 68 marks, there should be 20 that are directed towards **Context**.

Using the 34 questions within this book, it is quite easy to meet the first condition. The second one, however, is less easy to meet. The following selection of questions does meet both of these requirements:

AoS1	Question 5	8 marks
AoS1	Question 3	9 marks
AoS2	Question 18	8 marks
AoS2	Question 11	9 marks
AoS3	Question 22	9 marks
AoS3	Question 23	8 marks
AoS4	Question 27	9 marks
AoS4	Question 34	8 marks

HOW TO COMBINE QUESTIONS

This second selection has fewer marks based on contextual questions, as the majority of such questions from the first three AoS are included in the selection above.

AoS1	Question 5	8 marks
AoS1	Question 7	9 marks
AoS2	Question 12	8 marks
AoS2	Question 13	9 marks
AoS3	Question 21	8 marks
AoS3	Question 25	9 marks
AoS4	Question 32	9 marks
AoS4	Question 28	8 marks

It might also help teachers, when looking for specific examples of question types, to note that Questions 3, 7, 9, 10 and 16 contain examples where candidates are required to fill in missing notes from a melody.

Those that contain contextual questions are 1, 5, 11, 18, 22, 23, 27, 31, 32, 33 and 34.

Section B: Study pieces

Time: 30 minutes Section B total: 28 marks

Answer **Question 1** and **one** question from **Questions 2-4**.

Question 1

Area of Study 1: Western Classical tradition 1650–1910

Haydn: Symphony No. 101 – second movement, 'The Clock'

1. The timpani of Haydn's time were less advanced than those of today.

   Explain how this affects the music played by the timpani and how these instruments are notated in the score.

   _____

   _____

   [2 marks]

2. Identify **two** ways in which Haydn creates a sense of contrast between sections in this piece.

   _____

   _____

   [2 marks]

3. Identify **two** ways in which Haydn has structured the second movement of **Symphony No. 101.**

   _____

   _____

   [2 marks]

4. Explain how Haydn has used the musical elements to develop the original melody during the second movement of **Symphony No. 101.**

   _____

   _____

   _____

   _____

   _____

   _____

   _____

   _____

   [8 marks]

Total: 14 marks

SECTION B: STUDY PIECES

Question 2

Area of Study 2: Popular music

The Beatles: 'With a Little Help from My Friends', 'Lucy in the Sky with Diamonds', 'Within You Without You', from *Sergeant Pepper's Lonely Heart's Club Band*

1. Ringo Starr, who was not regarded as being a confident singer, sang the lead vocal on **'With a Little Help from My Friends'**.

   Identify **two** ways in which Lennon and McCartney wrote a vocal part suitable for such a vocalist.

   [2 marks]

2. **'With a Little Help from My Friends'** is introduced by a segue/link from the previous song (**'Sergeant Pepper's Lonely Hearts Club Band'**). This required the Beatles to modulate from C major to E major.

   Identify **two** ways in which this modulation is achieved.

   [2 marks]

3. Identify **two** ways in which panning is used in the recording of **'Lucy in the Sky with Diamonds'**.

   [2 marks]

4. Explain how musical elements associated with Indian music are used in **'Within You, Without You'**.

   [8 marks]

   Total: 14 marks

Question 3

Area of Study 3: Traditional music

Santana: 'Love of My Life', 'Migra', 'Smooth'

1. Identify **two** ways in which technology has been used on the vocals in **'Smooth'**.

   [2 marks]

2. Identify **two** ways in which the lead guitar interacts with other melody parts in **'Migra'**.

   [2 marks]

3. The final section of **'Love of My Life'** features no vocal and takes the form of an extended guitar solo.

   Identify **two** ways this guitar solo is different from previous sections.

   [2 marks]

4. Explain how musical elements associated with contemporary Latin music are used within **'Love of My Life'**.

   [8 marks]

   Total: 14 marks

SECTION B: STUDY PIECES

Question 4

Area of Study 4: Western Classical tradition since 1910

Aaron Copland: 'Saturday Night Waltz' and 'Hoe Down' from *Rodeo*

1. Identify **two** ways in which the opening of **'Hoe Down'** differs from the rest of the movement.

   _____

   _____ [2 marks]

2. **'Hoe Down'** is a movement from a larger work, called ***Rodeo***, which is set in the Wild West.

   Identify **two** ways in which the musical features of **'Hoe Down'** are suitable for a musical about cowboys and cowgirls.

   _____

   _____ [2 marks]

3. Identify **two** ways in which the music of **'Saturday Night Waltz'** develops during the movement.

   _____

   _____ [2 marks]

4. Explain how the elements of music are used to make **'Saturday Night Waltz'** and **'Hoe Down'** suitable for two very different styles of dance.

   _____

   _____

   _____

   _____

   _____

   _____

   _____

   _____ [8 marks]

   Total: 14 marks

Answers

Section A: Listening – unfamiliar music

Area of Study 1: Western Classical tradition 1650–1910

Question 1

1. violin(s) — 1 mark
2. w plagal — 1 mark
   x perfect — 1 mark
3. y octave — 1 mark
   z 5th — 1 mark
4. major — 1 mark
5. Any **three** of: — 3 marks
   - primary chords / I, IV, V / tonic, subdominant, dominant
   - inner pedal
   - pedal
   - movement in (parallel) 3rds
   - balanced phrases
   - short phrases
   - (mostly) stepwise movement
   - repetition (of melodic phrases)

   Any other valid point

   Total: 9 marks

Question 2

1. One mark for each of: — 3 marks
   - anacrusis
   - chromatic movement
   - triadic movement
2. D minor (allow dominant) — 1 mark
3. 5th — 1 mark
4. allegretto (allow allegro, moderato) — 1 mark
5. $\frac{3}{4}$, $\frac{3}{8}$ — 1 mark
6. perfect — 1 mark
7. (symphony) orchestra — 1 mark

Total: 9 marks

Question 3

1. oboe — 1 mark
2. 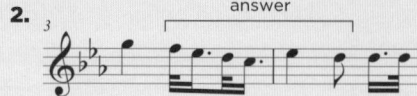 [musical notation excerpt marked "answer"]

   One mark for each correct note — 6 marks
   One mark for correct shape regardless of starting note
3. melody and accompaniment — 1 mark
4. major — 1 mark

Total: 9 marks

Question 4

1. bassoon — 1 mark
2. Any **two** of: — 2 marks
   - acciaccatura
   - appoggiatura
   - trill
   - turn
3. melody and accompaniment — 1 mark
4. strings and woodwinds — 1 mark
5. adagio / lento / largo — 1 mark
6. $\frac{4}{4}$ / $\frac{2}{4}$ / $\frac{2}{2}$ / C / ₵ — 1 mark
   (allow common time or split common time)
7. perfect — 1 mark
8. dominant — 1 mark

Total: 9 marks

Question 5

1. SATB — 1 mark
2. One mark for each of: — 2 marks
   - contrapuntal
   - imitative
3. B — 1 mark
4. D — 1 mark
5. Any **three** of: — 3 marks
   - primary chords / I, IV, V / tonic, subdominant, dominant
   - inner pedal
   - strings / string-based
   - harpsichord
   - continuo
   - cello (to emphasise the bass line)

   Any other valid point

Total: 8 marks

GCSE MUSIC LISTENING TESTS

Question 6

1. minor — 1 mark

2. Any **three** of: — 3 marks
- stepwise
- rising
- chromatic
- first two notes are on the same pitch
- last two notes are on the same pitch / tied

3. allegro / fast — 1 mark

4. homophonic — 1 mark

5. perfect — 1 mark

6. major — 1 mark

7. B — 1 mark

Total: 9 marks

Question 7

1. imperfect — 1 mark

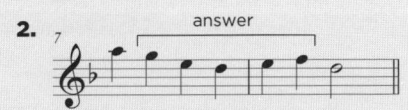

2. [musical notation]

One mark for each correct note — 5 marks
One mark for correct shape regardless of starting note

3. A^{1}A^2 BB A^{1}A^2 — 1 mark

4. Any **two** of: — 2 marks
- legato
- staccato
- accent / fp
- spread chord

Total: 9 marks

Question 8

1. major (1 mark) 6th (1 mark) — 2 marks

2. D — 1 mark

3. dominant 7th — 1 mark

4. andante / andantino / lento / moderato — 1 mark

5. One mark for each of: — 2 marks
- rallentando
- rubato

6. major — 1 mark

Total: 8 marks

Question 9

1. octaves — 1 mark

2. acciaccatura — 1 mark

3. 5th — 1 mark

4. [musical notation]

One mark for each correct note — 5 marks
One mark for correct shape regardless of starting note

5. legato — 1 mark

Total: 9 marks

Question 10

1. (church/pipe) organ – not electronic organ / (electric) keyboard — 1 mark

2. soprano — 1 mark

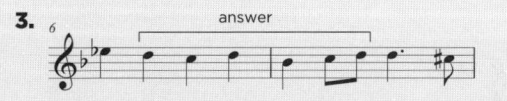

3. [musical notation]

One mark for each correct note — 6 marks
One mark for correct shape regardless of starting note

4. crescendo / cresc. / (they get) louder / (they) increase / go up — 1 mark

Total: 9 marks

Area of Study 2: Popular music

Question 11

1. piano — 1 mark

2. One mark for each of:
- stepwise — 1 mark
- downwards — 1 mark

3. note of anticipation — 1 mark

4. $\frac{4}{4}$ / $\frac{2}{4}$ / $\frac{2}{2}$ / C / $\cent$ — 1 mark
(allow common time or split common time) \

5. **One** of: — 1 mark
- strings
- percussion

6. Any **three** of: — 3 marks
- repetitive melodic line
- memorable melody
- short phrases
- some melodic decoration
  - mordent
  - pitch anticipation
  - portamento
- male and female voices
- vocal duet involved
- male voice answered by female

Any other valid point

Total: 9 marks

Question 12

1.
- x 3rd — 1 mark
- y 2nd — 1 mark
- z 3rd — 1 mark

2. flute(s) — 1 mark

3. pizz / pizzicato / plucked (**not** picked) — 1 mark

4. $\frac{3}{4}$ / $\frac{3}{8}$ / $\frac{3}{2}$ — 1 mark

5. **One** of: — 1 mark
- snare drum
- tambourine

6. 1st — 1 mark

Total: 8 marks

Question 13

1. C — 1 mark

2. six — 1 mark

3. none of them — 1 mark

4. glissando — 1 mark
power chords — 1 mark

5.
- $w = 4$ — 1 mark
- $x = 12$ — 1 mark
- $y = 13$ — 1 mark
- $z = 15$ or 16 — 1 mark

Total: 9 marks

Question 14

1. recorders — 1 mark

2. broken chords — 1 mark

3. lento / slow / fairly slow — 1 mark

4. stepwise (allow restricted / limited / narrow) — 1 mark

5. A — 1 mark

6. chromatic — 1 mark
descending — 1 mark

7. modal — 1 mark

Total: 8 marks

Question 15

1. penny whistle / tin whistle / (wooden) flute — 1 mark

2. strings — 1 mark

3. slow / moderately slow / andante / lento / adagio — 1 mark

4. Any **two** of: — 2 marks
- glissando
- (upper) mordent
- appoggiatura

5. $\frac{12}{8}$ or $\frac{6}{8}$ or $\frac{9}{8}$ or $\frac{3}{8}$ or $\frac{3}{4}$ — 1 mark

6. broken chords — 1 mark

7. 1st — 1 mark

8. minor — 1 mark

Total: 9 marks

Question 16

1. male voice choir — 1 mark
2. a cappella — 1 mark
   unison — 1 mark
3. *(notated melody with "answer" bracket)*

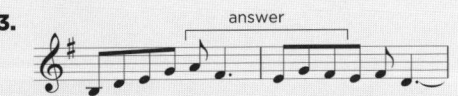

   One mark for each correct note — 6 marks
   One mark for correct shape regardless of starting note

   Total: 9 marks

Question 17

1. Any **five** of: — 5 marks

   Melody
   - mostly stepwise / conjunct
   - descending (overall)
   - overlaps after two beats at first
   - (then) overlaps after four beats
   - melodic line decorated (additional marks for details)
   - melismatic setting of the word
   - starts on the dominant / 5th note of the scale
   - ends on the tonic / 1st note of the scale

   Texture
   - melody and accompaniment
   - solo voice and accompaniment (at first)
   - backing voices added
   - parts move in parallel (3rds / 5ths)
   - overlapping parts lead to a contrapuntal / polyphonic texture

   Any other valid point under either heading

2. modal — 1 mark
3. second / second and fourth / off beat(s) / back beat(s) / weak beats — 1 mark
4. piano — 1 mark
5. 12/8 / 6/8 / 9/8 / 3/8 / 3/4 — 1 mark

   Total: 9 marks

Question 18

1. harp (allow acoustic or classical guitar, but not electric or bass / mandolin) — 1 mark
2. *(rhythm notation: rest, two quavers, rest, crotchet, barline)*

   1 mark for each correct note value, including the rest — 4 marks
   Where the rest has been omitted, the maximum mark which can be awarded is 2

3. melody and accompaniment — 1 mark
4. Any **three** of: — 3 marks

   Rhythm
   - steady beat
   - driving pulse
   - off-beat / syncopated accents / rhythm
   - 4/4

   Melody
   - repetitive melody
   - (fairly) narrow range
   - short phrase
   - memorable
   - singable

   Dynamics
   - loud (consistently)
   - suitable for a large venue (e.g. stadium / large hall)
   - "big" sound (use of amplifiers)

   Use of instruments / voices
   - main solo voice with melody
   - some use of portamento / glissando
   - backing vocals
   - drums used to provide beat / drive
   - strong / prominent bass (underpinning the texture / creating drive)

   Any other valid point

   Total: 9 marks

Area of Study 3: Traditional music

Question 19

1. One mark for each of: **3 marks**
   - blue notes
   - melisma
   - riff
2. twelve-bar blues — 1 mark
3. (acoustic) guitar — 1 mark
4. swing / boogie / shuffle — 1 mark
5. 4/4 / 2/4 / 2/2 / C / ¢ — 1 mark
   (allow common time or split common time)
6. Any **one** of: — 1 mark
   - pitch bend
   - picking
   - strumming
   - double-stopping

Total: 8 marks

Question 20

1. One mark for each of: **3 marks**
   - bar 2: dominant 7th
   - bar 4: minor
   - bar 7: dominant 7th
2. blues combo — 1 mark
3. muting / (con) sord / (con) sordino — 1 mark
4. swing / boogie / shuffle — 1 mark
5. 4/4 or 2/4 or 2/2 or C or ¢ — 1 mark
   (allow common time or split common time)
6. 90bpm / andante / moderato / lento / (quite) slow — 1 mark

Total: 8 marks

Question 21

1. delay (accept echo / ADT/automatic double tracking) — 1 mark
2. One mark for each of: **2 marks**
   - muting
   - skank
3. one-drop — 1 mark
4. reggae — 1 mark

5. Any **three** of: **3 marks**
   - call and response
   - homophonic
   - improvisation / ad lib
   - harmonies
   Any other valid point

Total: 8 marks

Question 22

1. a cappella — 1 mark
2. One mark for each of: **2 marks**
   - anacrusis
   - call and response
3. major — 1 mark
4. reverb — 1 mark
5. homophonic — 1 mark
6. Any **three** of: **3 marks**
   - syncopation
   - a cappella
   - overlapping melodies / dovetailing
   - harmonised voices
   - choral timbres
   Any other valid point

Total: 9 marks

Question 23

1. major — 1 mark
2. One mark for each of: **2 marks**
   - detached
   - syncopated
3. saxophone(s) — 1 mark
4. woodwind — 1 mark
5. Any **three** of: **3 marks**
   - brass (section)
   - bongos
   - congas
   - maracas
   - bass
   - all reference to the vocal 'grunts'
   Any other valid point

Total: 8 marks

Question 24

1. minor — 1 mark
2. One mark for each of: — 3 marks
   - arpeggio
   - son
   - sequence
3. melody and accompaniment — 1 mark
4. One mark for each of: — 3 marks
   - accordion
   - drum kit
   - electric guitar

Total: 8 marks

Question 25

1. One mark for each of: — 2 marks
   - descending
   - scale
2. minor — 1 mark
3. Any **three** of: — 3 marks
   - second verse adds bass
   - second verse adds tambourine
   - second verse adds backing vocals
   - crescendo in second verse / (gets/is) louder

   Any other valid point
4. melody and accompaniment — 1 mark
5. Any **two** of: — 2 marks
   - descending pitch
   - portamento / (vocal) slides / glissandi
   - 'swell' dynamics

   Any other valid point

Total: 9 marks

Question 26

1. Any **three** of: — 3 marks
   - arco
   - glissando
   - tremolo
2. rallentando / gets slower — 1 mark
3. three — 1 mark
4. ukulele — 1 mark
5. major — 1 mark
6. melody and accompaniment (accept homophonic) — 1 mark

Total: 8 marks

Area of Study 4: Western Classical tradition since 1910

Question 27

Excerpt A

1. bassoon(s) (allow bass clarinet) — 1 mark
2. timpani — 1 mark
3. $\frac{3}{4}$ — 1 mark
4. staccato — 1 mark
   syncopation — 1 mark

Excerpt B

5. Any **four** of: — 4 marks
   - (some) dissonance
   - lacks obvious chord progressions/cadences
   - lack of tonal centre
   - angular melody
   - uneven phrase lengths
   - lacks 'singable' melody (like **some** post-1910 music)
   - octatonic scale
   - individual instrumental timbres / solo instruments

   Any other valid point

Total: 9 marks

Question 28

1. One mark for each of: — 2 marks
   - brass
   - percussion
2. Any **two** of: — 2 marks
   - starts fortissimo/very loud
   - gets gradually quieter
   - forte/loud once the trumpet enters

   Any other valid point
3. Any **two** of: — 2 marks
   - horns / additional instruments in bars 16–19
   - melody is harmonised
   - texture becomes homophonic
   - higher register in 16–19

   Any other valid point

4. Any **two** of: 2 marks
   - brass
   - percussion
   - fanfare
   - 4ths
   - 5ths

   Any other valid point

   Total: 8 marks

Question 29
Excerpt A

1. (Scottish) bagpipes — 1 mark
2. F major — 1 mark
3. violins — 1 mark
4. andante / moderato / alla Marcia / at a walking speed / at a moderate speed / steadily — 1 mark

Excerpt B

5. quavers — 1 mark
   rubato — 1 mark
6. C — 1 mark
7. A¹A²A³B — 1 mark

Total: 8 marks

Question 30

1. harp — 1 mark
2. pedal — 1 mark
3. sequence — 1 mark
4. Any **two** of: 2 marks
   - starts slowly
   - speeds up / gets faster
   - slows down / gets slower
   - changes speed/tempo or speed/tempo varies

   Any other valid point
5. Any **two** of: 2 marks
   - starts quietly
   - gets louder / crescendo
   - gets quieter / diminuendo
   - dynamics vary

   Any other valid point
6. (symphony) orchestra — 1 mark

Total: 8 marks

Question 31

1. bassoon — 1 mark
2. One mark for each of: 2 marks
   - arco
   - pizzicato
3. moderato — 1 mark
4. Any **one** of: 1 mark
   - staccato
   - 'stab' chords
   - sforzando

   Any other valid point
5. drone — 1 mark
6. Any **two** of: 2 marks
   - chromaticism
   - tonal ambiguity
   - syncopation
   - repetition
   - re-harmonised folk melodies (nationalism)

   Any other valid point

Total: 8 marks

Question 32
Excerpt A

1. strings — 1 mark
2. start quietly — 1 mark
   get louder / crescendo — 1 mark
3. oboe — 1 mark
4. (con) arco — 1 mark
   pizz / pizzicato / plucked (**not** 'picked') — 1 mark

Excerpt B

5. Any **three** of: 3 marks
   - lively
   - suitable for dancing
   - has characteristics of gipsy music
   - semiquaver-dotted quaver rhythm / scotch snap
   - (D) minor scale used
   - cimbalom / hammered dulcimer
   - strings / violins (further association with gipsy music)

   Any other valid point

Total: 9 marks

Question 33

1. minimalism — 1 mark
2. One mark for each of: — 2 marks
   - picking
   - strumming
3. polyphonic — 1 mark
4. multi-tracking (overdubbing) — 1 mark
5. presto / molto allegro / very fast / 192 bpm — 1 mark
6. Any **two** of: — 2 marks
   - repetition
   - note addition / subtraction
   - resultant melody
   - ostinato
   - electric / amplified instruments

   Any other valid point

   Total: 8 marks

Question 34

1. strings — 1 mark
2. Any **two** of: — 2 marks
   - (con) arco
   - pizz / pizzicato / plucked (**not** picked)
   - harmonics
   - double-stopping
3. *p*   *p* — 1 mark
4. **Four** from the below with at least one from each heading: — 4 marks

   Melody
   - short melodic patterns repeated / overlapping
   - additive melodic ideas / extra note(s) added after several repetitions

   Harmony
   - doesn't move much / quite static / little variety
   - harmonies build up / cumulative harmonies

   Rhythm
   - repetitive rhythmic patterns
   - variety of rhythmic ideas
   - additive rhythmic ideas / extra note(s) added after several repetitions
   - lacks a strong sense of pulse
   - overlapping rhythms

   Any other valid point

   Ensure answers relate only to these three headings

   Ensure there is no repetition across headings

   Total: 8 marks

Section B: Study pieces

Question 1

Area of Study 1: Western Classical tradition 1650–1910

Haydn: Symphony No. 101 – second movement, 'The Clock'

1. Any **two** of: — 2 marks
   - only two notes / only D and G / only tonic and dominant
   - the parts are notated without key signatures
   - the A timpani has to be re-tuned to G for this movement

   Any other valid point

2. Any **two** of: — 2 marks
   - varying between major and minor keys
   - dramatic contrast of dynamics
   - contrasting timbres (woodwind and strings dominate in one section, brass in the other)

   Any other valid point

3. Any **two** of: — 2 marks
   - ternary / sonata form
   - two main melodies used throughout
   - use of a silent bar

   Any other valid point

4. **Extended response** — 8 marks

   Level of response:

   7–8 A comprehensive response that is consistently coherent and logically structured

   5–6 A wide-ranging response that is mostly coherent and well structured

   3–4 A relevant response despite some inaccuracy/omission and weaknesses in terms of coherency and structure

   1–2 A limited response with some significant inaccuracy/omission and a lack of clarity

   0   no work submitted or worthy of credit

   Indicative content

   Extended responses could include the following:

   Melody
   - sequence (additional credit for detail)

Dynamics
- alternating between piano and forte (additional credit for detail)

Rhythm
- rhythmic variation (additional credit for detail)
- rhythmic variation of accompaniment (sextuplets and triplets)

Harmony
- modulation (one mark for a general point *or* one mark for identifying specific modulations)
- inverted pedal in the oboe part
- use of chromatic chords (specifically German augmented 6th); additional credit for detail

Texture
- antiphonal writing (additional credit for detail)
- additional contrasting lines (accept brief polyphony/descant)

Timbre
- adding/changing instruments (additional credit for detail)
- changing accompaniment patterns (additional credit for detail)
- violas change to playing triple-stopped chords (additional credit for explanation of 'triple-stopped chords')

Any other valid point

Total: 14 marks

Question 2

Area of Study 2: Popular music

The Beatles: 'With a Little Help from My Friends', 'Lucy in the Sky with Diamonds', 'Within You Without You', from *Sergeant Pepper's Lonely Heart's Club Band*

1. Any **two** of: 2 marks
   - narrow range
   - call and response with other singers
   - syllabic lyric setting
   - phrases on one note

   Any other valid point

2. Any **two** of: 2 marks
   - use of rising parallel chords (C–D–E)
   - use of a rising scale in the melody
   - use of a guitar 'turnaround' phrase to prepare a perfect cadence (E–A–B)

   Any other valid point

3. Any **two** of: 2 marks
   - extreme panning
   - two guitars – one panned extreme left, one panned extreme right
   - organ panned left
   - drum kit panned left
   - vocals panned centre
   - bass panned centre

   Any other valid point

4. **Extended response**   8 marks

   Level of response:

   7–8 A comprehensive response that is consistently coherent and logically structured

   5–6 A wide-ranging response that is mostly coherent and well structured

   3–4 A relevant response despite some inaccuracy/omission and weaknesses in terms of coherency and structure

   1–2 A limited response with some significant inaccuracy/omission and a lack of clarity

   0 no work submitted or worthy of credit

   Indicative content

   Extended responses could include the following:

   Instrumentation
   - sitar
   - tambura
   - dilruba
   - swarmandal
   - tabla

   Melody
   - raga (accept mixolydian mode)
   - doubling / ornamenting the melody
   - pitch bends
   - glissandi

   Harmony
   - drone
   - built on one main chord

   Texture
   - heterophonic texture (between vocal and dilruba) (additional credit for detail)

   Rhythm/metre
   - tala
   - (accept ambiguous metre / changing metre / irregular metre, etc.) (additional credit for detail)

   Any other valid point

   Total: 14 marks

Question 3

Area of Study 3: Traditional music
Santana: 'Love of My Life', 'Migra', 'Smooth'

1. One mark for each of: 2 marks
   - telephone voice (narrow-band EQ)
   - mild distortion
   - double tracking (automatic double tracking/ADT)
   - additional vocals by lead vocalist
   - delay (accept echo)
   - reverb

   Any other valid point

2. One mark for each of: 2 marks
   - call and response (with voice)
   - homophonic (harmony) with horns
   - links sections together
   - guitar solo

   Any other valid point

3. One mark for each of: 2 marks
   - faster tempo
   - faster harmonic pace/harmonic rhythm
   - no call and response
   - more overt use of Latin rhythms
   - (much) longer phrase lengths

   Any other valid point

4. Extended response   8 marks

   Level of response:

   7–8 A comprehensive response that is consistently coherent and logically structured

   5–6 A wide-ranging response that is mostly coherent and well structured

   3–4 A relevant response despite some inaccuracy/omission and weaknesses in terms of coherency and structure

   1–2 A limited response with some significant inaccuracy/omission and a lack of clarity

   0 no work submitted or worthy of credit

   Indicative content

   Extended responses could include the following:

   Instrumentation
   - Latin percussion
   - trap drums
   - cowbell
   - cajon
   - guiro
   - timbales
   - congas

   Rhythm/metre/tempo
   - syncopation
   - Latin rhythms
   - improvisation
   - dance section / livelier at the end
   - ballad / slow(er) section(s)

   Melody
   - pitch bend
   - anacrusis
   - two- and four-bar phrases
   - call and response (between both voice and guitar and two guitars)
   - improvisation
   - use of modes

   Texture
   - occasional polyphonic writing between guitar and voice
   - melody and accompaniment

   Any other valid point

       Total: 14 marks

Question 4

Area of Study 4: Western Classical tradition since 1910
Aaron Copland: 'Saturday Night Waltz' and 'Hoe Down' from *Rodeo*

1. Any **two** of: 2 marks
   - fanfare
   - repeated note / chord
   - antiphonal writing

   Any other valid point

2. Any **two** of: 2 marks
   - use of percussion to imitate the sound of a horse trotting
   - a trotting bassline (based on steady ascending melodic 3rds)
   - wide harmonic intervals (to create sense of open spaces)
   - lively dance / barn dance
   - simple duple metre

   Any other valid point

GCSE MUSIC LISTENING TESTS

3. Any **two** of: 2 marks
- ambiguity of metre
- accompaniment becomes less waltz-like
- texture gradually becomes more homophonic
- original theme returns at the end

Any other valid point

4. Extended response   8 marks

Level of response:

7–8 A comprehensive response that is consistently coherent and logically structured

5–6 A wide-ranging response that is mostly coherent and well structured

3–4 A relevant response despite some inaccuracy/omission and weaknesses in terms of coherency and structure

1–2 A limited response with some significant inaccuracy/omission and a lack of clarity

0 no work submitted or worthy of credit

Indicative content

Extended responses could include the following:

Metre/tempo
- 'Hoe Down': duple time
- 'Hoe Down': fast / lively tempo
- 'Hoe Down': varying tempi allows for broad range of dancing
- 'SNW': mostly triple time
- 'SNW': slow and stately tempo
- 'SNW': shifting sense of metre

Melody
- 'Hoe Down': rapid swirling / barn dance / lively melodies
- 'SNW': longer phrase lengths

Texture
- 'Hoe Down': melody and accompaniment / homophonic
- 'Hoe Down': stark contrast between sections
- 'Hoe Down': steady, driving bass contrasting with bass-light sections
- 'SNW': variety of homophonic and polyphonic textures
- 'SNW': call and response between flutes (to imply different characters in the dance)

Timbre
- 'Hoe Down': arco strings
- 'SNW': variation of arco and pizzicato strings
- 'SNW': light timbres contrasting with 'raw' / accented (or similar) opening

Any other valid point

Total: 14 marks

Track listings

Section A

Question 1
Mozart: Symphony No. 39, second movement

(recorded with repeat)
Mozart Symphonies 38–41
Scottish Chamber Orchestra/Mackerras
Linn Records CKD 308
CD1 Track 6
0'00" – 0'41"

Question 2
Mozart: Symphony No. 40, third movement

(recorded with repeat)
Mozart Symphonies 38–41
Scottish Chamber Orchestra/Mackerras
Linn Records CKD 308
CD2 Track 3
0'00" – 0'26"

Question 3
Beethoven Symphony No. 3, second movement

Beethoven: 9 Symphonies/Overtures
Berlin Philharmonic/Karajan
Deutsche Grammophon CD 415 066-2
CD2 Track 2
0'34" – 1'07"

Question 4
Mozart: Bassoon Concerto, second movement

Mozart: Concerto for Flute and Harp/
Sinfonia Concertante for Winds/
Bassoon Concerto
Britten Sinfonia/Cleobury
Sony Clasical 88697891092
Track 8
0'34" – 1'49"

Question 5
Handel: The King Shall Rejoice

Handel Coronation Anthems
English Chamber Orchestra/Willcocks
Decca Ovation 421 150-2
Track 10
0'45.5" – 1'16"

Question 6
Handel: Messiah, Part 3 No. 46, Chorus

'Since By Man Came Death', Grave and Allegro
Handel: *Messiah*
Choir of New College, Oxford/
Academy of Ancient Music/Higginbottom
Naxos 8.570131-32
CD2 Track 23
0'00" – 0'52"

Question 7
Schumann: *Album für die Jugend* No. 12 'Volksliedchen'

Ammara
Arts 477568
Track 9
0'00" – 1'20"

Question 8
Chopin: Prelude Op. 28 No. 7 in A

Chopin Preludes/Ashkenazy
Decca
Track 7
0'00" – 0'56"

Question 9
Verdi: Requiem, Agnus Dei

Verdi: *Requiem Mass*
Chorus and Orchestra of the Opera House,
Rome/Serafin
Naxos 8.110159
Track 14
0'45" – 1'31"

Question 10
Fauré: Requiem, Kyrie

Faure Requiem
Schola Cantorum of Oxford/
Oxford Camerata/Summerly
Naxos 8.550765
Track 1
3'13.75" – 4'03.25"

Question 11
Menken: *Little Shop of Horrors*, 'Suddenly Seymour'

Little Shop of Horrors – Music from the
Original Motion Picture Soundtrack
Geffen Records GFLD 19289
Track 9
0'41" – 1'45"

GCSE MUSIC LISTENING TESTS

Question 12
Bernstein: West Side Story, 'I Feel Pretty'
Sony SK 48211
Track 10
0'53" – 1'18"

Question 13
The Kinks: 'All Day and All of the Night'
The Best of the Kinks
Castle Select SELCD 560
Track 2
0'00" – 0'38"

Question 14
Led Zeppelin: 'Stairway to Heaven'
Mothership
Atlantic 8122-79961-5
CD1 Track 13
0'26" – 1'21"

Question 15, Excerpt A
Howard Shore: *Lord of the Rings* (Main Theme)
The Ultimate Classical Box
Sony/BMG 88697206502
CD5 Track 11
1'48" – 2'18"

Question 15, Excerpt B
Michael Nyman: *The Piano*
The Ultimate Classical Box
Sony/BMG 88697206502
CD5 Track 5
0'09" – 0'26"

Question 16
***Halo*: Original Soundtrack, Opening Suite**
Cadiz Music SE-2002-2
Track 1
0'37" – 1'07"

Question 17
Alicia Keys: 'Fallin''
Songs in A Minor
Music for Pleasure 74321928892 8
Track 4
1'55" – 2'26"

Question 18
Florence and the Machine: 'Between Two Lungs'
Dog Days are Over
Island Records 275 381 1
CD1 Track 1
0'24" – 1'00"

Question 19
Robert Johnson: 'Sweet Home Chicago'
1'03" – 1'31"

Question 20
Bessie Smith: 'Nobody Knows You When You're Down and Out'
0'56" – 2'04"

Question 21
Bob Marley: 'One Love'
Legend
Island/Tuff and Gong 548 904-2
0'25" – 1'00"

Question 22
Paul Simon: 'Diamonds on the Soles of Her Shoes'
Graceland
Legacy Recordings
0'00" – 0'56"

Question 23
Pérez Prado: 'Mambo No. 5'
RCA Victor
0'00" – 0'46"

Question 24
Shakira: 'La Tortura'
Fijacion Oral, Vol. 1
Epic
0'18" – 0'51"

Question 25
Mumford & Sons: 'Thistle and Weeds'
Sigh No More
Universal/Island Records
1'03" – 2'15"

GCSE MUSIC LISTENING TESTS

Question 26
Noah and the Whale: '5 Years' Time'
Peaceful, The World Lays Me Down
Virgin EMI
0'00" – 0'52"

Question 27, Excerpt A
Aaron Copland: *El Salon Mexico*
Appalachian Spring, Billy the Kid, Danzon Cubana, El Salon Mexico
London Symphony Orchestra/Dorati
Decca
1'18.675" – 1'40.025"

Question 27, Excerpt B
Aaron Copland: Organ Symphony, Prelude
Ives: Concord Symphony, Copland: Organ Symphony
San Francisco Symphony Orchestra/ Tilson Thomas/Jacobs
Track 5
0'00" – 0'49"

Question 28
Aaron Copland: *Fanfare for the Common Man*
El Salon Mexico
London Symphony Orchestra/Copland
Sony
0'00" – 1'13"

Question 29, Excerpt A
Peter Maxwell Davies: *An Orkney Wedding, with Sunrise*
Peter Maxwell Davies: A Celebration of Scotland
Treasure Island DKP(CD)9070
Track 1
11'00" – 11'24"

Question 29, Excerpt B
Malcolm Arnold: *Concerto for Guitar and Small Orchestra*, Allegro
Arnold: Guitar Concerto; English Dances; Symphony for Brass
English Chamber Orchestra/Wordsworth
Decca
Track 1
1'22" – 1'46"

Question 30
Benjamin Britten: 'Storm Interlude', (*Peter Grimes*, Act One: VII. Interlude II)
Britten: Peter Grimes
Royal Opera House Orchestra/Britten
Decca
2'40" – 3'22"

Question 31
Béla Bartók: 'Dance Suite' (Sz 77:1, Moderato)
Bartok: Concerto for Orchestra, Dance Suite, The Miraculous Mandarin
London Symphony Orchestra/Solti
Decca
0'00" – 0'40"

Question 32, Excerpt A
Béla Bartók: *Concerto for Orchestra* – fourth movement, *Intermezzo interrotto*
Classic Masterpieces
Budapest Philharmonic Orchestra/Saccani
BPOL Live 1015
Track 10
0'00" – 0'16"

Question 32, Excerpt B
Kodály: Háry *Janos Suite* – fifth movement, *Intermezzo*
Classic Masterpieces
Budapest Philharmonic Orchestra/Saccani
BPOL Live 1015
Track 5
0'22" – 0'50"

Question 33
Steve Reich: *Electric Counterpoint*, 3rd movement, Fast
Different Trains/Electric Counterpoint
Nonesuch
0'33" – 1'23"

Question 34
John Adams: *Shaker Loops* – third movement, *Loops and Verses*
Shaker Loops
Bournemouth Symphony/Alsop
Naxos 8.559031
Track 6
0'47" – 1'34"

Glossary

A cappella Unaccompanied singing; from the Italian meaning 'in the chapel style', this term originally applied to church music, but is now used for all genres of music.

Accent A stress on a certain beat or particular note.

Acciaccatura (pronounced *at-chak-ka-too-rah*) An ornament printed as a small note with a slash through its tail, which is played as quickly as possible before the main note that follows it.

Adagio A slow tempo.

Alberti bass A type of broken chord accompaniment, often on a keyboard instrument.

Alla marcia In the style of a march.

Allegro A fast tempo.

Anacrusis One or more weak-beat notes before the first strong beat of a phrase, which is often called a 'pick up' in pop music.

Andante A moderately slow tempo.

Antiphony, Antiphonal A musical texture where two groups of musicians take it in turns to play.

Appoggiatura A melodic ornament where a neighbouring note (that sounds dissonant) is sounded for a measured period of time before the main note of the melody.

Arco An instruction for string players to use the bow, after playing pizzicato.

Arpeggio The notes of a standard chord played one after another, in ascending or descending order, that is, the first, third, fifth and eighth notes of a scale.

Articulation The amount of space between the notes, so whether the notes are played very detached (staccato), or joined together (legato).

Atonal Music without an obvious key.

Augmentation A proportionate increase in the note lengths of a melody, for example, when two quavers and a crotchet are augmented they become two crotchets and a minim; the opposite of **diminution**.

Automatic double-tracking (ADT) A technological effect and recording technique used by The Beatles to double the sound of voices or instruments. This doubled effect (similar to double-tracking) created a richer sound.

Backbeat A term used in pop music to describe accenting the normally weak second and fourth beats in $\frac{4}{4}$ time.

Blue notes In blues music, notes added to a scale which are usually a flattened 3rd or flattened 7th.

Boogie woogie A type of blues, often with a piano accompaniment and a driving rhythm.

Broken or spread chord A chord in which the notes are sounded individually, rather all being played exactly together. An arpeggio is a type of broken chord.

Cadence A pair of chords which mark the end of a musical statement.

Call and response Vocal music in which a soloist sings a phrase to which a group of singers respond. Mostly found in African music, but also in jazz and pop music.

Chromatic Notes that don't belong to the current key; the opposite of **diatonic.**

Col legno Played with the wood of a bow, rather than the hair, producing a dry sound.

Con sordino Played with a mute on the instrument.

Conjunct A style of melodic writing in which each note is a step away from the previous one.

Continuo Accompanying part in instrumental music of the Baroque period. Played by a bass instrument (such as a cello) and a harmony instrument (such as a harpsichord).

Contrapuntal Music that uses counterpoint, a texture where two or more melodic lines are played together at the same time.

Descant A counter melody sung above the main melody line.

Diatonic Music using just the notes of the home key; the opposite of **chromatic**.

Diminution The opposite of **augmentation**: a proportionate reduction in the note lengths of a melody, for example, when two quavers and crotchet are diminished they become two semiquavers and a quaver.

Disjunct A style of melodic writing including many leaps between one note and the next; opposite of **conjunct**.

Dissonant A combination of notes producing a clashing sound when played together; opposite of **consonant.**

Dominant 7th A triad with an added 7th note which is a whole tone away from the tonic, so in G major it would consist of G, B, D and F. It can also be written as V^7.

Double- and triple-stopping Two or three notes played at the same time on a stringed instrument.

Doubling More than one part playing the same line, either in unison or an octave apart.

Drone One or more notes held or repeated throughout an extended passage of music.

Finger-picking A guitar-playing technique where notes are plucked individually, rather than strummed as part of a chord.

Glissando A slide from one pitch to another.

Hammer-on (ho) On a string instrument (often the guitar), this involves 'hammering' a finger on to the fretboard, causing a note to sound. This allows guitarists to play fast, legato phrases.

Hemiola A rhythmic device in which two groups of three beats (*strong-weak-weak, strong-weak-weak*) are performed as three groups of two (*strong-weak, strong-weak, strong-weak*).

Heterophony The simultaneous performance of a melody and a variation of the melody.

Homophony, homophonic A musical texture in which all parts (melody and accompaniment) move in similar rhythm creating a chordal effect.

Imitative, or imitation A device where the melody in one part is copied a few notes later in a different part, often at a different pitch, with the two parts overlapping.

Improvisation Music made up by the performer as they play, and not notated by the composer.

Interval The distance between two pitches: count the letter names between the notes including the first and last, so C to G is a 5th.

Inversion When a melody is inverted, the intervals between the notes are the same as the original phrase, but they move in the opposite direction to the original – so a pitch will rise instead of falling, or the other way round.

Inverted pedal See **pedal note**; an inverted pedal note sounds higher than the harmonies beneath it, instead of lower.

Largo A very slow tempo.

Legato Played smoothly, without breaks between the notes.

Lento A slow tempo.

Marcato Marked, or accented playing.

Melisma A group of notes sung to the same syllable.

Moderato A moderate tempo.

Modes, modal An alternative series of scales to the diatonic major and minor scales, often used in traditional music.

Modulation The process of changing key midway through a piece.

Monophony Music consisting of a single unaccompanied melody line.

Mute Device attached to an instrument to soften the tone and produce a different timbre, for string and brass instruments; see **con sordino**.

Note addition Where notes are added in to a repeating phrase.

Off-beat A note that sounds between the main beats of a composition.

Ostinato A rhythmic, melodic or harmonic pattern repeated many times in succession (similar to a riff in pop music).

Palm mute (pm) A playing technique for guitarists where the side of the picking hand is rested on the strings to dampen the sound.

Pedal note A sustained or regularly repeated note, usually heard in the bass, while the harmony above changes between various chords. Usually the pedal note is the tonic or dominant.

Pentatonic scale A scale of only five notes.

Pitch bend A short slide up or down to the main note.

Pizzicato An instruction for string players to pluck the string instead of using the bow.

Polyphony A musical texture where two or more parts move independently of one another.

Portamento Sliding from one pitch to another.

Power chord In pop and rock music, a chord that consists of the root and the fifth, especially on electric guitars and often used with distortion.

Presto A very fast tempo.

Raga A scale pattern or melodic motif used as the basis for melodic improvisation in Indian classical music.

Rallentando Slowing down.

Relative major/minor A pair of keys which share the same key signature, one major and one minor: for example, the relative minor of F major is D minor, and the relative major of D minor is F major.

Reverb Short for reverberation, an effect used to alter music so that it sounds as if recorded in a reverberant, echoey space.

Riff In jazz, pop and rock, a short, catchy melodic or rhythmic idea repeated throughout a song.

Rubato Flexibility with the notated rhythms, shortening some and lengthening others.

Scale Eight notes, making up all the notes in a key. The degrees of the scale have the following names:
- I   Tonic
- II   Supertonic
- III   Mediant
- IV   Subdominant
- V   Dominant
- VI   Submediant
- VII   Leading note
- VIII   Tonic

Sequence The immediate repetition of a motif or phrase at a different pitch.

Sforzando Strongly accented note, indicated with the sign *sf*.

Shuffle Similar to a swing rhythm, but with a much stronger triplet feel.

Skank The up-stroke, off-beat strumming pattern that accompanies ska and (some) reggae music; also refers to a dance that accompanies reggae music.

Son A musical form, or type of song, originating from Cuba, with a distinctive clave rhythm pattern, and where the only accompaniment is percussion or rhythmic instruments.

Sonata form The most common structure for the first movement (and sometimes other movements) of compositions in the Classical style, comprising exposition, development and recapitulation.

Spiccato A bowing technique for string players where the bow is bounced on the string, creating very detached notes.

Staccato Short, detached playing, with gaps between the notes.

Suspension A note repeated or sustained over a change in harmony, creating a dissonance, and then resolving onto a note within the key.

Swung rhythm In jazz and blues style, the first quaver of a pair will often be played slightly longer than the second one.

Syncopation The effect created when accented notes are sounded off the beat or on weak beats, often with rests on some of the strong beats.

Tierce de Picardie A major chord used to end a piece of music in a minor key.

Tremolo A musical effect created by the rapid repetition of a single note.

Triadic A melody based on the notes of a triad. A triad is a chord of the 1st, 3rd and 5th notes of a scale, either major or minor.

Turn An ornament, consisting of the note above the written note, the written note, the note below the written note, and the written note once again.

Tutti A marking meaning 'All', so the whole ensemble should play.

Una corda The soft pedal on a piano, so that only one string plays rather than three.

Unison Two or more people performing the same note or melody; in a choir when everyone is singing the same melody, even though the men are singing an octave lower than the women.

Vivace A lively tempo.

Whole-tone scale A scale where there is a whole tone between all the notes, with no semitones as there would be in a conventional scale.

Printed music copyrights

'All Day And All Of The Night'
Words & Music by Ray Davies, © Copyright 1964 Edward Kassner Music Company Limited.
All Rights Reserved. International Copyright Secured.

Opening Suite (From *Halo*)
Music by Martin O'Donnell & Michael Salvatori, © Copyright 2002 Microsoft Music Publishing,
Warner/Chappell North America Limited. All Rights Reserved. International Copyright Secured.

'Diamonds On The Soles Of Her Shoes'
Words & Music by Paul Simon, © Copyright 1986 Paul Simon (BMI). All Rights Reserved.
International Copyright Secured. Reprinted by Permission of Music Sales Corporation (ASCAP).

'Thistle and Weeds'
Words & Music by Mumford & Sons, © Copyright 2009 Universal Music Publishing Limited.
All Rights Reserved. International Copyright Secured.

Fanfare For The Common Man
Music by Aaron Copland, © Copyright 1942 Boosey and Hawkes Inc.,
Boosey & Hawkes Music Publishing Limited. All Rights Reserved. International Copyright Secured.

Concerto For Guitar Op. 67
Music by Malcolm Arnold, © Copyright 1959 Paterson's Publications Limited.
All Rights Reserved. International Copyright Secured.

Mechanical copyrights

'Suddenly Seymour' (Menken/Ashman)
Warner/Chappell North America Limited/Universal/
MCA Music Limited

'I Feel Pretty' (Sondheim/Bernstein)
Universal Music Publishing Limited

'All Day And All Of The Night' (Davies)
Edward Kassner Music Co Ltd

'Stairway to Heaven' (Plant/Page)
Warner/Chappell North America Limited

Lord of the Rings (Main Theme) (Shore)
Universal/MCA Music Limited

The Piano (Nyman)
Chester Music

Halo (Opening Suite) (Salvatori/O'Donnell)
Warner/Chappell North America Limited

'Fallin'' (Augello Cook)
EMI Music Publishing Ltd

'Between Two Lungs' (Welch/Summers)
Universal Music Publishing Limited

'Sweet Home Chicago' (Johnson)
Kobalt Music Publishing Limited

'One Love' (Marley)
Blue Mountain Music Ltd

'Diamonds on the Soles of Her Shoes' (Simon)
Universal/MCA Music Limited

'Mambo No. 5' (Prado)
Latin-American Music Publishing Ltd

'La Tortura' (Ripoll/Ochoa)
Sony/ATV Harmony UK

'Thistle and Weeds' (Mumford/Dwane/Lovett/Marshall)
Universal Music Publishing Limited

'5 Years' Time' (Fink)
Universal Music Publishing Limited

El Salon Mexico (Copland)
Boosey & Hawkes Music Publishers Ltd

Organ Concerto (Copland)
Boosey & Hawkes Music Publishers Ltd

Fanfare for the Common Man (Copland)
Boosey & Hawkes Music Publishers Ltd

An Orkney Wedding with Sunrise (Maxwell Davies)
Boosey & Hawkes Music Publishers Ltd

Concerto for Guitar and Small Orchestra (Arnold)
Patersons Publications Ltd/Malcolm Arnold

Peter Grimes (Slater/Britten)
Boosey & Hawkes Music Publishers Ltd

Háry Janos Suite (Kodály)
Universal Edition AG (Wien)/Zoltan Kodály

Electric Counterpoint (Reich)
Hendon Music Ltd

Shaker Loops III Loops and Verses (Adams)
G Schirmer Ltd

How to download your music tracks

1. Carefully remove your Download Card from the inside back cover of this book.

2. On the back of the card is your unique access code. Enter this at www.musicsalesdownloads.com

TO REDEEM THIS CARD VISIT
www.musicsalesdownloads.com

ENTER ACCESS CODE:
XXXXXXXXX

Download Cards are powered by Dropcards.
User must accept terms at dropcards.com/terms
which are adopted by The Music Sales Group.
Not redeemable for cash. Void where prohibited or restricted by law.

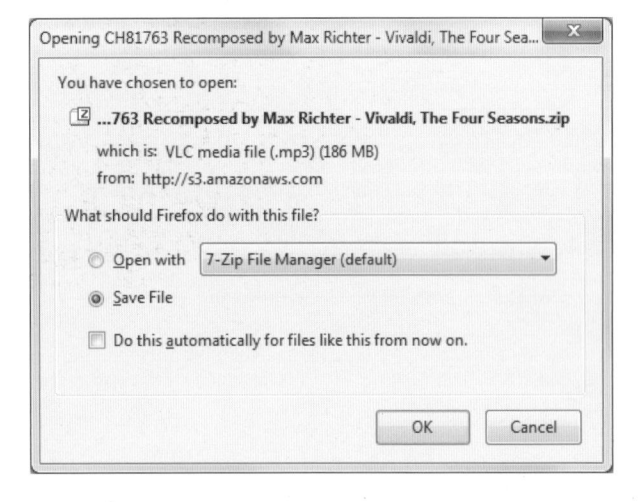

3. Follow the instructions to save your files to your computer*. That's it!

*Appearance of download manager will vary depending upon operating system and web browser.
In case of difficulty when downloading files, please contact dropcards.com/help
Card missing? Please contact music@musicsales.co.uk